DROPPING SEEDS

DROPPING SEEDS

A DAILY DEVOTIONAL WORKBOOK

DARLENE NELSON

XULON ELITE

Xulon Press Elite
2301 Lucien Way #415
Maitland, FL 32751
407.339.4217
www.xulonpress.com

Paperback ISBN-13: 978-1-66286-937-2
Ebook ISBN-13: 978-1-66286-938-9

PREFACE:

This devotional workbook aims to strengthen your relationship with our Father and become more Christlike. I hope that it allows us to tap into His unique Holy Spirit. We can draw on this gift to transform our hearts and minds so the world will not doubt who we serve by the fruit we bear. The title comes from watching my parents work in our family garden each year. They would go along each row "dropping seeds," hoping they would take root and produce "good fruit" for our family.

I want to thank Jehovah God, my Lord and Savior Jesus Christ, and the Holy Spirit for my inspiration. To God be all the glory!

I want to dedicate this book to two inspirational pastors in my life:

To Pastor Claudell Anderson: Thank you for giving me numerous opportunities to do the two things I love the most, write and talk about the Lord.

And to Pastor Jesse McLendon: Thank you for always believing I could.

Introduction:

This devotional workbook is to improve your relationship with God through faith in His Word and your works. The devotional aspect is for anyone who wants a better understanding of God's Word. The Bible verses are in parentheses and are no more than two. Primarily, I have used the English Standard Version (ESV). There is a summary of the verses given afterward. They also consist of only a few sentences for quick and easy reading. Each day reflects a particular fruit of the Spirit. The first letter or letters of the fruit identifies it. There is a prayer that corresponds to each fruit. The workbook portion has a broad application of the fruit and space to record how you applied that fruit in your day.

The application should be specific enough to enhance your life or the life/lives of someone else. For example, January 1st is (J) for joy. The broad application is to find joy in today. Your application may be to go for a walk with a close friend. Another example, June 25th, is (LS) for long-suffering. The broad application is to count on His presence. Your application might be to read one of your favorite scriptures to help you through a difficult time. It's crucial to note that this workbook is not used as a scoring system, competition, or test. It is as personal as your relationship with God and will be used to purposefully look for opportunities to glorify Him through His Holy Spirit.

(F) FAITH

Jehovah God, holy is your name. Your kingdom will come, and your will shall be done here on earth as it is in heaven. Today Lord, I ask your Holy Spirit to increase my faith. I stand on my Christian belief in the death, burial, and resurrection of my Lord and Savior, Jesus Christ. I pray my faith grows as I study your Word, anticipate your promises, and witness your works. I will encourage others along the way to do the same. I pray my works are a testament to my trust in you. You are my protector. I have faith in your wisdom, grace, and mercy. I look to you as the source of everything and realize you eagerly wait to supply my every need and desire according to your will. I rest in your capable hands, confident that I am on the right path. I loyally wait for your return. I will forever appreciate your gift of faith because it leads to eternal life. I will always put you first and uplift your sacred name. These things I pray in your faithful Son Jesus Christ's name, Amen.

(GE) GENTLENESS

Jehovah God, holy is your name. Your kingdom will come, and your will shall be done here on earth as it is in heaven. Today Lord, I ask your Holy Spirit's help to remain kind. I will use my words to build others up, not tear them down. I will be considerate of others not only through my words but through my actions. I will look for opportunities to help others with their immediate needs. I will do this by going beyond my comfort zone and reaching out to those I consider strangers. Please increase my mercy, understanding, and forgiveness as I seek to care for others. Give me what I need to be kind yet strong enough for the task. I will continue to be kindhearted as I speak your Word so that I may not be a stumbling block to anyone's salvation. Help me remember that I was once lost before you showed me love and kindness. I pray we all unite and come together to glorify your name. I will always put you first. These things I pray in your kind Son Jesus Christ's name, Amen.

(GO) GOODNESS

Jehovah God, holy is your name. Your kingdom will come, and your will shall be done here on earth as it is in heaven. Today Lord, I ask your Holy Spirit's help in exercising goodness. In today's world with all the concerns about crime and safety, it's easy to shy away from being good to others. But Lord, I vow not to dwell on the evils of this world. I pray for protection from it. I choose to focus on you and your goodness. Thank you for the integrity and light you've shown us through your Son Jesus. I want to intervene for others as He did for me. I want to tell everyone about your goodness. Help me speak for those who can't speak for themselves and treat others with dignity and respect. Teach me to give special consideration to my brothers and sisters in Christ. Please help me do good deeds for the building of your kingdom. Please give me the patience and strength to stay the course. Remind me that the greatest good we can do in this world is to be obedient to you. I will surround myself with the righteous and do good while I can. I will always put you first and uplift your sacred name. These things I pray in your good Son Jesus Christ's name, Amen.

(J) JOY

Jehovah God, holy is your name. Your kingdom will come, and your will shall be done here on earth as it is in heaven. Today Lord, I ask your Holy Spirit to sustain my joy. I never want to lose my joy because you sent your Son Jesus so I may have eternal life through faith in Him. I am glad you love me and that I belong to you. I find joy in the peace you give me. I have joy because I can rely on your Word. I rejoice in the simplest of things and when you open the floodgates of heaven. Each day brings me joy because it is a blessing you saw fit to breathe life into me. This day is even more special because it gives me another opportunity to uplift, glorify, and magnify your name! Today I will find joy in loving and giving to others. I rejoice no matter what because you hold the power of heaven and earth in your hands. I am glad to know you and be in your presence as I come to you in prayer. I am happy when I fellowship with others who know you as I do. I rejoice with you and the saints when another one of us runs from the devil into your open arms. I am happy to be obedient, seek your guidance, and tell others of your awesomeness. I will always put you first and uplift your sacred name. These things I pray in your triumphant Son Jesus Christ's name, Amen.

(LS) LONG-SUFFERING

Jehovah God, holy is your name. Your kingdom will come, and your will shall be done here on earth as it is in heaven. Today Lord, I ask for your Holy Spirit's strength to endure. Guide me down the path of tolerance, patience, and acceptance. Help me Lord to resist situations where I may want to harbor bitterness and anger due to feeling provoked or used. Stay close to me as I walk through the day's trials. Order my steps according to your purpose. Give me a heart that forgives man's shortcomings as you do my own. See that I become a person of second chances because you are a God of many. Allow me to know the difference between Godly discernment and judging others. Lord, give me a heart that acknowledges and trusts your timeline, not mine. I diligently seek your will through your Word and boldly proclaim it to others. Help me to remember that my hardships are not in vain if they are for Christ's sake and the hope of salvation. Continue to comfort me as I go through the day and help me to rely on your promises. I will always put you first and uplift your sacred name. These things I pray in your patient Son Jesus Christ's name, Amen.

(L) LOVE

Jehovah God, holy is your name. Your kingdom will come, and your will shall be done here on earth as it is in heaven. Today Lord, I ask your Holy Spirit to teach me to be more loving. I love and trust you as the head of my life. So I thank you and look to you as the supreme example of unconditional love. I pray to look beyond others' faults to examine their needs, just as you did for me when you sent your Son Jesus Christ. I want your light to shine through me as I go about the day so the world will want to know the kind of God I serve. When I see my brothers and sisters fall, I pray for you to catch them instead of trying to analyze their circumstances. Help me to advise my fellow man lovingly. Instill in me your unique understanding so I can freely love the seemingly unlovable, give to those in need, and combat hatred with compassion. Remind me to tell others of the love you have for them. I value all your many blessings. I will always put you first and uplift your sacred name. These things I pray in your loving Son Jesus Christ's name, Amen.

(M) MEEKNESS

Jehovah God, holy is your name. Your kingdom will come, and your will shall be done here on earth as it is in heaven. Today Lord, I ask your Holy Spirit to keep me humble. Through humility, I can repent, receive forgiveness, and heal. I yield to your way and purpose for my life. I can do this because as my creator, you know me better than I know myself. Because I submit to you, your grace is always present in my life. Lord, please show me ways I can be courteous to others today. Squash my pride so I can receive your Word and apply it as I deal with others. Allow me to serve you, whether behind the scenes or in front of a crowd. Please help me not to think highly of myself in case I forget to praise you for all I am. Keep me mindful of your hand in every aspect of my life. Teach me to speak gently to others as I tell them about you being the source of my salvation. I will always put you first and uplift your sacred name. These things I pray in your humble Son Jesus Christ's name, Amen.

(P) PEACE

Jehovah God, holy is your name. Your kingdom will come, and your will shall be done here on earth as it is in heaven. Today Lord, I seek your Holy Spirit to remain at peace. I know you're able because you already sent your Son Jesus who delivered perfect harmony to an imperfect, sinful world. I pray for that peace to last as I wait for His return. I leave all my worries and troubles in your capable hands. Remove all turmoil and confusion from my life. Clear my mind from all doubt and fear. I will search for your acceptance instead of the world's consent. I want to be the one who tries to look for common ground among my brothers and sisters without compromising righteousness. I ask that I never seek revenge on others. I want to have the blessing of quiet rest. Let me find peace in your Word as I learn to serve you better daily. I will always put you first and uplift your sacred name. These things I pray in your peaceful Son Jesus Christ's name, Amen.

(T) TEMPERANCE

Jehovah God, holy is your name. Your kingdom will come, and your will shall be done here on earth as it is in heaven. Today Lord, I ask your Holy Spirit's help in being more disciplined. To do this, I will cling to you and what is pleasing in your sight. Anything contrary to that should bother my soul. I acknowledge I belong to you (and you to me), so I will conduct myself in the most righteous way possible. I will look for ways to serve you as I pray and study your Word. I understand the sacrifice Jesus made to set us free from sin was not for us to become enslaved again. I trust the boundaries for my life that you have laid out in your Word because I know you are a God that keeps nothing excellent and perfect from me. Denying the desires of the flesh and this world is not a burden but a benefit. Please continue to give me the courage and strength to overcome the challenges of the day. I won't take the easy way out when it comes to temptations. I will remember how far you have brought me. I will flee from any form of sexual immorality because a sin against the body is a sin against you. Grant me wisdom to walk in righteousness. Bridle my tongue. I will always put you first and uplift your sacred name. These things I pray in your obedient Son Jesus Christ's name, Amen.

JANUARY 1:

(J) Psalm 118:24 (This is the day the Lord has made; let us rejoice and be glad in it.) Every day is a blessing from the Lord. It is a new and unique experience. For that opportunity, we should be delighted. It is another chance to do the will of God.

- Broad application: Find joy in today.
- Your application:

_____
_____
_____
_____
_____
_____
_____
_____
_____
_____
_____
_____
_____
_____
_____
_____
_____
_____
_____
_____

JANUARY 2:

(F) John 11:40 (Jesus said to her, "Did I not tell you that if you believed, you would see the glory of God?") Our faith in God grows every time we take Him at His Word. He does not lie. God wants us to see Him in all His glory. Our continued faith in Him allows this to happen.

- Broad application: See His glory.
- Your application:

_____

_____

_____

_____

_____

_____

_____

_____

_____

_____

_____

_____

_____

_____

_____

_____

_____

_____

_____

JANUARY 3:

(F) 2 Corinthians 5:7 (For we walk by faith, not sight.) Having faith in our heavenly Father is the basis of our Christian walk. And as we walk, our hope is fueled by things that are not often physically seen. Our hope lies in the spiritual realm. Our eyes are not needed there, but our hearts are.

- Broad application: See with your heart.
- Your application:

_____
_____
_____
_____
_____
_____
_____
_____
_____
_____
_____
_____
_____
_____
_____
_____
_____
_____
_____
_____

JANUARY 4:

(GE) Proverbs 15:1 (A soft answer turns wrath away, but a harsh word stirs anger.) It is just as important to know how to say something as it is to know what to say. Both skills are God-given. A gentle tone of voice shows we are open to a resolution. A harsh tone promotes conflict.

- Broad application: Watch how you speak.
- Your application:

_____
_____
_____
_____
_____
_____
_____
_____
_____
_____
_____
_____
_____
_____
_____
_____
_____
_____
_____
_____
_____

JANUARY 5:

(GO) Galatians 6:1 (Brothers, if anyone sins, you who are spiritual should restore him in a spirit of gentleness. Keep watch on yourself, lest you too be tempted.) We are to intervene when we see our Christian brothers and sisters fall short. We should expect the same considerate intervention when we fall short. But we must be careful. Our sinful nature may override our intentions as we deal with the sins of others.

- Broad application: Do good; practice caution.
- Your application:

_____
_____
_____
_____
_____
_____
_____
_____
_____
_____
_____
_____
_____
_____
_____
_____
_____
_____
_____
_____

January 6:

(LS) Psalm 86:15 (But you, O Lord, are a God merciful and gracious, slow to anger and abounding in steadfast love and faithfulness.) Do we ever have moments when we must stop and be in awe of God's amazing grace and mercy? And it is fresh and new every day! His love for us is never-ending. He is truly a God of many chances.

- Broad application: Give someone another chance.
- Your application:

_____
_____
_____
_____
_____
_____
_____
_____
_____
_____
_____
_____
_____
_____
_____
_____
_____
_____
_____
_____
_____

January 7:

(L) Genesis 2:15 (The Lord God took the man and put him in the garden of Eden to work it and keep it) Each day we are blessed to be alive allows us to love. And when we exhibit that love, it is not just toward each other. We should love everything the Lord our God has made. We must remember to be good stewards of the blessings He gives us.

- Broad application: Look after your blessings.
- Your application:

_____
_____
_____
_____
_____
_____
_____
_____
_____
_____
_____
_____
_____
_____
_____
_____
_____
_____
_____
_____

JANUARY 8:

(M) Titus 3:2 (...to speak evil of no one, avoid quarreling, be gentle, and show perfect courtesy toward all people.) We do not need to insult others. Because when we do, it just leads to strife. We should keep the peace and be courteous to everyone. It is the way of the Lord.

- Broad application: Speak no evil.
- Your application:

_____
_____
_____
_____
_____
_____
_____
_____
_____
_____
_____
_____
_____
_____
_____
_____
_____
_____
_____
_____

JANUARY 9:

(P) 1 Peter 5:7 (...casting all your anxieties on him because he cares for you.) Chaos takes a toll on our entire well-being. It can steal our joy, therefore denying us peace. God is not a God of confusion. We look forward to going home so we can be at rest.

- Broad application: Cast all on Him.
- Your application:

_____
_____
_____
_____
_____
_____
_____
_____
_____
_____
_____
_____
_____
_____
_____
_____
_____
_____
_____
_____
_____
_____

JANUARY 10:

(T) Titus 2:12 (...training us to renounce ungodliness and worldly passions, and to live self-controlled, upright, and godly lives in the present age.) As children of God, we must turn away from sinful lifestyles. Sin should disturb us as much as it does our Creator. The world can never be our example. We should always follow Jesus's example.

- Broad application: Do Godly things.
- Your application:

_____
_____
_____
_____
_____
_____
_____
_____
_____
_____
_____
_____
_____
_____
_____
_____
_____
_____
_____
_____

JANUARY 11:

(F) Romans 10:17 (So faith comes from hearing, and hearing through the Word of Christ.) The Great Commission is not just for our clergy. Each one of us gets instructions to spread the Word of God. Through His Word, we get to know Him. By knowing Him, we learn to believe in Him.

- Broad application: Let someone hear you.
- Your application:

_____

_____

_____

_____

_____

_____

_____

_____

_____

_____

_____

_____

_____

_____

_____

_____

_____

_____

_____

JANUARY 12:

(F) James 1:3 (For you know that the testing of your faith produces steadfastness.) We go through many trials and tribulations here on earth. Some are of our own making; some are life's circumstances. Some are of the devil. When we get tested, our faith in God can help us to stand in the midst of them. Victory comes from having faith in God to see us through.

- Broad application: Be unmovable.
- Your application:

_____
_____
_____
_____
_____
_____
_____
_____
_____
_____
_____
_____
_____
_____
_____
_____
_____
_____
_____
_____

JANUARY 13:

(GE) Philippians 4:5 (Let your reasonableness be known to everyone. The Lord is at hand.) Show the whole world our gentle spirit. Be kind and mild-mannered. The Lord is watching. He will be pleased.

- Broad application: Be considerate of others.
- Your application:

_____
_____
_____
_____
_____
_____
_____
_____
_____
_____
_____
_____
_____
_____
_____
_____
_____
_____
_____
_____

JANUARY 14:

(GO) Romans 12:9 (Let love be genuine. Abhor what is evil; hold fast to what is good.) God is love. Real love is full of the goodness of the Lord. Evil is something to despise and avoid. We should hold tight to what is good and holy, no matter what.

- Broad application: To love is good.
- Your application:

_____

_____

_____

_____

_____

_____

_____

_____

_____

_____

_____

_____

_____

_____

_____

_____

_____

_____

_____

_____

_____

_____

JANUARY 15:

(J) John 15:11 ("These things I have spoken to you, that my joy may be in you, and that your joy may be complete.") True pleasure can only come from knowing God. It is not like happiness, which is fleeting. Joy sustains us during life's disappointments and trials. The glass is more than half full when God's joy is in us.

- Broad application: Fill up!
- Your application:

_____
_____
_____
_____
_____
_____
_____
_____
_____
_____
_____
_____
_____
_____
_____
_____
_____
_____
_____
_____
_____
_____

JANUARY 16:

(LS) Romans 8:28 (All things work together for good for those who love him, and he calls according to his purpose.) God has a specific design for us all. As part of that design comes life's inevitable bouts of joy and pain. But through it all, we hold on to the promise of a better day. That day is when we will be with Him eternally.

- Broad application: Count it all good.
- Your application:

_____
_____
_____
_____
_____
_____
_____
_____
_____
_____
_____
_____
_____
_____
_____
_____
_____
_____
_____
_____

JANUARY 17:

(L) Proverbs 19:17 (Whoever is generous to the poor lends to the Lord, and he will repay him for his deed.) The Bible tells us it is simply a part of our sin-sick world. The poor are going to always be with us. But the Bible also tells us to take every opportunity to help those who are less fortunate. In doing so, we glorify God and will reap His reward.

- Broad application: Give generously to others.
- Your application:

_____

_____

_____

_____

_____

_____

_____

_____

_____

_____

_____

_____

_____

_____

_____

_____

_____

_____

_____

JANUARY 18:

(M) Ecclesiastes 10:4 (If the ruler's anger rises against you, do not leave your place, for calmness will lay great offenses to rest.) Humility is not a weakness when dealing with offensive behavior from those in authority. It allows the Holy Spirit to give us much-needed courage and strength. We then use both to reach a level of calmness to fight another day. When we practice this, humility becomes an admirable trait.

- Broad application: Take the high road.
- Your application:

_____
_____
_____
_____
_____
_____
_____
_____
_____
_____
_____
_____
_____
_____
_____
_____
_____
_____

JANUARY 19:

(P) Hebrews 12:14 (Strive for peace with everyone, and for the holiness without which no one will see the Lord.) Only the devil enjoys seeing us in turmoil. God commands us to love each other so we can live harmoniously. It is an accurate indicator of our allegiance to Him. We can't see Him spiritually or be with Him eternally without peace.

- Broad application: Get along with others.
- Your application:

_____

_____

_____

_____

_____

_____

_____

_____

_____

_____

_____

_____

_____

_____

_____

_____

_____

_____

_____

_____

January 20:

(T) Proverbs 25:28 (A man without self-control is like a city broken into and left without walls.) There are things we should and should not do. "Anything goes" is not the Christian way. There are boundaries. We need walls.

- Broad application: Practice self-control.
- Your application:

_____

_____

_____

_____

_____

_____

_____

_____

_____

_____

_____

_____

_____

_____

_____

_____

_____

_____

_____

JANUARY 21:

(F) Proverbs 3:5 (Trust in the Lord with all your heart, and do not lean on your understanding.) We can never be as wise as our almighty God. So we may not truly understand <u>His</u> plans for us. But He does because He made us. He knows us.

- Broad application: Trust your maker.
- Your application:

January 22:

(F) Hebrews 11:6 (And without faith it is impossible to please him, for whoever would draw near to God must believe he exists and that he rewards those who seek him.) We cannot please God if we do not acknowledge that He exists. His name is "Elohim," "Yahweh," and "I Am." He is real. Those who seek Him get rewarded.

- Broad application: Call Him by name.
- Your application:

_____
_____
_____
_____
_____
_____
_____
_____
_____
_____
_____
_____
_____
_____
_____
_____
_____
_____
_____

JANUARY 23:

(GE) Proverbs 16:24 (Gracious words are like a honeycomb, sweetness to the soul and health to the body.) God gives the righteous ones wisdom. We use that wisdom to discern what is right and wrong. Using kind words is food for our body and soul. It is the right thing to do.

- Broad application: Speak sweet.
- Your application:

_____

_____

_____

_____

_____

_____

_____

_____

_____

_____

_____

_____

_____

_____

_____

_____

_____

_____

_____

_____

January 24:

(GO) Galatians 6:10 (So then, as we have the opportunity, let us do good to everyone, especially those of the household of faith.) As we minister to the world, let us not forget to minister to and support each other. Those who follow the Lord are first with Him. We should also put our Christian brothers and sisters first. We all share the same Father.

- Broad application: Put family first.
- Your application:

_____
_____
_____
_____
_____
_____
_____
_____
_____
_____
_____
_____
_____
_____
_____
_____
_____
_____
_____
_____

JANUARY 25:

(J) 1 Peter 1:8 (Though you have not seen him, you love him. Though you do not now see him, you believe in him and rejoice with joy that is inexpressible and filled with glory.) We will never see our Father with the naked eye, yet we love him anyway. Our faith in Him fuels that love. That faith gives us a joy we can't describe. Glory to His name.

- Broad application: Praise Him!
- Your application:

_____
_____
_____
_____
_____
_____
_____
_____
_____
_____
_____
_____
_____
_____
_____
_____
_____
_____
_____
_____

JANUARY 26:

(LS) Romans 2:4 (Or do you presume on the riches of his kindness, forbearance, and patience, not knowing that God's kindness will lead you to repentance?) God is slow to anger. He is tolerant of our shortcomings. But do not think it is for nothing. He is loving enough to give us plenty of opportunities to repent.

- Broad application: Practice His ways.
- Your application:

_____
_____
_____
_____
_____
_____
_____
_____
_____
_____
_____
_____
_____
_____
_____
_____
_____
_____
_____

JANUARY 27:

(L) Colossians 3:14 (And above all these put on love, which binds everything together in perfect harmony.) The character of a Christian shows the ability and desire to love. We can not let our light shine without it. We can not be consistent in our righteousness without it. It is the glue that holds us together.

- Broad application: Love. Love. Love again.
- Your application:

_____

_____

_____

_____

_____

_____

_____

_____

_____

_____

_____

_____

_____

_____

_____

_____

_____

_____

_____

JANUARY 28:

(M) Psalm 25:9 (He leads the humble in what is right and teaches the humble his way.) God promises to guide the meek. And through His guidance, we learn what is spiritually correct. His ways are righteous. We become moral when we follow Him.

- Broad application: Submit and follow.
- Your application:

_____
_____
_____
_____
_____
_____
_____
_____
_____
_____
_____
_____
_____
_____
_____
_____
_____
_____
_____
_____
_____

JANUARY 29:

(P) Colossians 3:15 (And let the peace of Christ rule in your hearts, to which God called us to be in one body. And be thankful.) When we allow Christ to rule in our hearts, peace is evident. We can have disagreements, but the goal is to be united in His will. We should thank God for showing us the way to achieve this. Without Him, it is not possible.

- Broad application: Show me the way.
- Your application:

_____
_____
_____
_____
_____
_____
_____
_____
_____
_____
_____
_____
_____
_____
_____
_____
_____
_____
_____
_____

JANUARY 30:

(T) 1 Corinthians 9:27 (But I discipline my body and keep it under control, lest after preaching to others I should be disqualified.) When we minister to others, we need to be ready for adversities. This Christian race requires conditioning. We do not want to find ourselves undeserving of the task. We must keep our eyes on the finish line.

- Broad application: Stay ready; stay focused.
- Your application:

_____

_____

_____

_____

_____

_____

_____

_____

_____

_____

_____

_____

_____

_____

_____

_____

_____

_____

_____

JANUARY 31:

(F) 1 John 5:4 (For everyone born of God overcomes the world. And this is the victory that has overcome the world, faith.) If we believe Jesus is the Son of God, then we are born of God. Confidence in the Son is having faith in the Father. God is the supreme ruler over the earth. We can withstand anything through faith in Him.

- Broad application: Claim the victory.
- Your application:

_____

_____

_____

_____

_____

_____

_____

_____

_____

_____

_____

_____

_____

_____

_____

_____

_____

_____

_____

_____

_____

FEBRUARY 1:

(F) Ephesians 2:8 (For by grace you have been saved through faith. And this is not your own doing; it is the gift of God.) By having faith in God, we receive His amazing grace. We cannot say we do anything to earn it. Salvation is His eternal gift to us. We do the work of the Lord because of that salvation.

- Broad application: Don't boast about yourself.
- Your persona application:

_____

_____

_____

_____

_____

_____

_____

_____

_____

_____

_____

_____

_____

_____

_____

_____

_____

_____

_____

_____

February 2:

(GE) Colossians 3:12 (Put on then, as God's chosen ones, holy and beloved, compassionate hearts, kindness, humility, meekness, and patience.) We are God's people. We are made righteous and have love because of this. So we should get dressed in kindness and gentleness every day, just as we put on our clothes. It should be a part of our daily routine.

- Broad application: Dress appropriately.
- Your application:

_____
_____
_____
_____
_____
_____
_____
_____
_____
_____
_____
_____
_____
_____
_____
_____
_____
_____
_____

FEBRUARY 3:

(GO) Psalm 27:13: (I believe I shall look upon the Lord in the land of the living!) God is good now and forever. We do not have to wait for eternal life to be in the presence of God. Our faith in Him also brings deliverance here on earth. He is God for the living.

- Broad application: Look around for God.
- Your application:

_____

_____

_____

_____

_____

_____

_____

_____

_____

_____

_____

_____

_____

_____

_____

_____

_____

_____

_____

_____

FEBRUARY 4:

(J) Psalm 94:19 (When the cares of my heart are many, your consolations cheer my soul.) Many things might concern us on a day-to-day basis. We can be anxious about things such as the demands of our jobs, financial obligations, and childcare. But when we trust in the Lord, we know where our support lies. Our soul finds continued comfort in Him.

- Broad application: Lean on the Lord.
- Your application:

_____

_____

_____

_____

_____

_____

_____

_____

_____

_____

_____

_____

_____

_____

_____

_____

_____

_____

_____

FEBRUARY 5:

(LS) 1 Corinthians 2:9 (He says, "What no eye has seen, nor ear heard, nor the heart of man imagined, what God has prepared for those who love him.") This world holds many mysteries. Some of them we may never know. But God's gift of wisdom is not one of those mysteries. He reveals His Word to the true believer through His Holy Spirit in due time.

- Broad application: Patiently seek Him.
- Your application:

_____

_____

_____

_____

_____

_____

_____

_____

_____

_____

_____

_____

_____

_____

_____

_____

_____

_____

_____

_____

FEBRUARY 6:

(L) 1 Corinthians 16:14 (Let all you do start with love.) Starting with love seems like such a simple thing. Simple, yet hard to do without the Holy Spirit guiding us. Love is a heart thing. We need Jesus in our hearts.

- Broad application: Examine your heart.
- Your application:

_____

_____

_____

_____

_____

_____

_____

_____

_____

_____

_____

_____

_____

_____

_____

_____

_____

_____

_____

_____

_____

_____

FEBRUARY 7:

(M) James 4:6 (But he gives more grace. Therefore, it says, "God opposes the proud but gives grace to the humble.") Being full of pride is the work of the devil. We do not have God's grace if we are prideful and of the world. And His grace gives us more than the world ever could. Being humble gives us access to abundant grace.

- Broad application: Desire more grace.
- Your application:

_____

_____

_____

_____

_____

_____

_____

_____

_____

_____

_____

_____

_____

_____

_____

_____

_____

_____

_____

_____

FEBRUARY 8:

(P) Ephesians 4:3 (...eager to maintain the unity of the Spirit in the bond of peace.) There is one Lord, one faith, and one baptism. There is one God and Father of all, one hope. There is one body, one Spirit. This unity of the Spirit is also seen among God's people when we are at peace.

- Broad application: Strive for peace.
- Your application:

_____

_____

_____

_____

_____

_____

_____

_____

_____

_____

_____

_____

_____

_____

_____

_____

_____

_____

_____

February 9:

(T) Proverbs 25:16 (If you have found honey, eat only enough for you, lest you have your fill of it and vomit it.) Christians must have restraint. It is what sets us apart from the world. Even those things which are enjoyable can be a problem. Too much can become toxic if we overindulge.

- Broad application: Know your limit.
- Your application:

_____

_____

_____

_____

_____

_____

_____

_____

_____

_____

_____

_____

_____

_____

_____

_____

_____

_____

_____

_____

FEBRUARY 10:

(F) James 2:24 (You see that a person receives justification by works and not by faith alone.) Having faith in God produces work for God. They go hand in hand. A person shows authenticity in his Christian walk when we see his dedication and work in action. Faith can move us.

- Broad application: Show up for service.
- Your application:

_____

_____

_____

_____

_____

_____

_____

_____

_____

_____

_____

_____

_____

_____

_____

_____

_____

_____

_____

FEBRUARY 11:

(F) Mark 11:24 ("Therefore I tell you, whatever you ask in prayer, believe that you have received it, and it will be yours.") We make our requests and concerns known to God in prayer. We go to Him in prayer because we know who is in control of everything. Whatever we ask is in His ability to give. If we believe it, we will receive it.

- Broad application: Believe. Receive.
- Your application:

_____

_____

_____

_____

_____

_____

_____

_____

_____

_____

_____

_____

_____

_____

_____

_____

_____

_____

_____

FEBRUARY 12:

(GE) 1 Timothy 6:11 (But as for you, O man of God, flee these things. Pursue righteousness, godliness, faith, love, steadfastness, gentleness.) We must fight the good fight. And in doing so, sometimes our strategy is to flee evil and go in another direction. So we choose the path according to His will. Gentleness is His will.

- Broad application: Pursue kindness.
- Your application:

_____

_____

_____

_____

_____

_____

_____

_____

_____

_____

_____

_____

_____

_____

_____

_____

_____

_____

_____

February 13:

(GO) Psalm 25:7 (Remember not the sins of my youth or my transgressions; according to your steadfast love, remember me, for the sake of your goodness, O LORD!) What a blessing to know that the Lord forgives us of our sins. It is an added assurance that He does not hold the childish sins we committed in the past against us. The goodness of God makes this possible. This verse alone can be our simple prayer.

- Broad application: Know God's goodness.
- Your application:

_____

_____

_____

_____

_____

_____

_____

_____

_____

_____

_____

_____

_____

_____

_____

_____

_____

_____

FEBRUARY 14:

(J) John 16:22 ("So also you have sorrow now, but I will see you again, and your hearts will rejoice, and no one will take your joy from you.") We will have sorrows and disappointments in life. And knowing the Lord will see us through. But there will come a time when joy never leaves us. We will rejoice forever in His presence!

- Broad application: Pray for eternal joy.
- Your application:

_____

_____

_____

_____

_____

_____

_____

_____

_____

_____

_____

_____

_____

_____

_____

_____

_____

_____

FEBRUARY 15:

(LS) Psalm 37:10 (In just a little while, the wicked will be no more; though you look carefully at his place, he will not be there.) It may seem like a long time to us, but God's timetable is not man's timetable. The devil can only move about the earth at the Lord's discretion. Justice and judgment will come. The devil will have no part in God's kingdom.

- Broad application: Wait on the Lord.
- Your application:

_____
_____
_____
_____
_____
_____
_____
_____
_____
_____
_____
_____
_____
_____
_____
_____
_____
_____

FEBRUARY 16:

(L) 1 John 4:19 (We love because he first loved us.) It is easy to love when love is shown to us first. God created us out of love for us. When sin separated us from that love, He sent His Son, Jesus, to redeem us. We love Jesus because we know the price He paid.

- Broad application: Love first.
- Your application:

_____

_____

_____

_____

_____

_____

_____

_____

_____

_____

_____

_____

_____

_____

_____

_____

_____

_____

_____

_____

FEBRUARY 17:

(M) 1Peter 5:5 (Likewise, you who are younger, be subject to the elders. Clothe yourselves, all of you, with humility toward one another, for "God opposes the proud but gives grace to the humble.) In this Christian walk, we are sure to have Christian elders. Those of us who are young in age or faith can learn from them what it means to be selfless. Wherever we are in our journey, pride has no place in serving God. His love and grace can only abound when we humble ourselves.

- Broad application: Rejoice in your humility.
- Your application:

_____

_____

_____

_____

_____

_____

_____

_____

_____

_____

_____

_____

_____

_____

_____

_____

_____

_____

FEBRUARY 18:

(P) 1 Thessalonians 5:15 (See that no one repays anyone evil for evil, but always seek to do good to one another and everyone.) It is not the Christian way to do evil when people do evil acts to us. That way of thinking robs us of our peace. We are responsible for always seeking to do good deeds for each other. The final judgment is for the Lord.

- Broad application: Don't look for revenge.
- Your application:

_____

_____

_____

_____

_____

_____

_____

_____

_____

_____

_____

_____

_____

_____

_____

_____

_____

_____

_____

_____

FEBRUARY 19:

(T) Romans 12:1 (I appeal to you brothers, by the mercies of God, to present your bodies as a living sacrifice, holy and acceptable to God, which is your spiritual worship.) Through God's grace and mercy, we belong to Him as He belongs to us. Therefore, we can offer up our bodies as living sacrifices. By doing so, He can work through us. Our righteous conduct is our ultimate worship.

- Broad application: Conduct yourself accordingly.
- Your application:

FEBRUARY 20:

(F) Mark 9:23 (And Jesus said to him, "If you can'! All things are possible for one who believes.") Sometimes it may seem as if things are impossible. We may see ourselves in situations or circumstances where we see no way out. Or, in our minds, we can not grasp any earthly solutions. But we must remember that God specializes in impossible things if only we believe.

- Broad application: Believe the impossible!
- Your application:

_____
_____
_____
_____
_____
_____
_____
_____
_____
_____
_____
_____
_____
_____
_____
_____
_____
_____

FEBRUARY 21:

(F) Hebrews 11:11 (By faith, Sarah herself received power to conceive, even when she was past the age, since she considered him faithful who had promised.) Sarah was ninety years old when she had the son promised her....90! She was, of course, way past her childbearing years, according to man. But Sarah was a woman of faith. She knew God would do what He said He was going to do.

- Broad application: Believe in His promises.
- Your application:

_____

_____

_____

_____

_____

_____

_____

_____

_____

_____

_____

_____

_____

_____

_____

_____

_____

_____

_____

FEBRUARY 22:

(GE) Isaiah 40:11 (He will tend his flock like a shepherd; he will gather the lambs in his arms, carry them in his bosom, and gently lead those with young.) The Lord will take care of His own. He will draw us to Him and comfort us. He is mighty yet gentle. Like Jesus, be a good shepherd.

- Broad application: Be solid, yet gentle.
- Your application:

_____
_____
_____
_____
_____
_____
_____
_____
_____
_____
_____
_____
_____
_____
_____
_____
_____
_____
_____
_____

FEBRUARY 23:

(GO) 1 Corinthians 10:23 (All things are lawful, but not all things are helpful. All things are legal, but not all things build up.) Good deeds are desirable, but not all are beneficial to kingdom building. Good deeds are needed, but not all are for the glory of God. Pray to know the difference. These are the ones that are in line with the will of God.

- Broad application: Glorify Him.
- Your application:

_____
_____
_____
_____
_____
_____
_____
_____
_____
_____
_____
_____
_____
_____
_____
_____
_____
_____

FEBRUARY 24:

(J) Psalm 16:11 (You tell me the path of life; in your presence, there is fullness of joy; at your right hand are pleasures forever.) God has shown us the way. Jesus is the light. We can be glad because of who He is. We will undoubtedly rejoice forever when we can spend eternity with our Father in heaven.

- Broad application: Be of good cheer.
- Your application:

_____

_____

_____

_____

_____

_____

_____

_____

_____

_____

_____

_____

_____

_____

_____

_____

_____

_____

_____

_____

FEBRUARY 25:

(LS) 2 Corinthians 4:17 (This light momentary affliction prepares us for an eternal weight of glory beyond all comparison.) The things we encounter here on earth can be challenging. But we must remember they are temporary. And they are preparing us for eternal life beyond anything we can imagine. Our lightweight troubles will not compare to the fullness of our glory in heaven with our Father.

- Broad application: Take heaven over earth.
- Your application:

_____

_____

_____

_____

_____

_____

_____

_____

_____

_____

_____

_____

_____

_____

_____

_____

_____

_____

FEBRUARY 26:

(L) 1 Corinthians 13:13 (So now faith, hope, and love abide, these three; but the greatest of these is love.) We believe in God. We long to be near Him. But nothing keeps us closer to Him than our love for Him. Through that love, He increases as we show that same love to others.

- Broad application: Glorify God with love.
- Your application:

_____

_____

_____

_____

_____

_____

_____

_____

_____

_____

_____

_____

_____

_____

_____

_____

_____

_____

_____

_____

FEBRUARY 27:

(M) 2 Samuel 22:28 (You save a humble people, but your eyes are on the haughty to bring them down.) God loves those who are willing to look to Him and His purpose. He cares for those who humble themselves and set aside their agendas. So He is unhappy when we use our energy to bring others down. We then become unfit for kingdom building.

- Broad application: Be about God's business.
- Your application:

_____
_____
_____
_____
_____
_____
_____
_____
_____
_____
_____
_____
_____
_____
_____
_____
_____
_____
_____

FEBRUARY 28:

(P) Proverbs 12:20 (Deceit is in the heart of those who devise evil, but those who plan peace have joy.) Having an evil spirit leads to conflict. There is no rest when someone practices deception and dishonesty. Evil doesn't produce peace. But anyone whose objective is peace will find joy in the Lord.

- Broad application: Find peace and joy.
- Your application:

_____
_____
_____
_____
_____
_____
_____
_____
_____
_____
_____
_____
_____
_____
_____
_____
_____
_____
_____
_____

MARCH 1:

(T) Colossians 3:10 (...and have put on the new self, which renews in knowledge after the image of its creator.) Once converted, we are no longer who we used to be. When we "put on the new self," it is a conscious decision to know more about our Savior. And as we seek to know and understand Him, we want to be more like Him. We deny our ways and cling to His.

- Broad application: Imitate Jesus.
- Your application:

_____

_____

_____

_____

_____

_____

_____

_____

_____

_____

_____

_____

_____

_____

_____

_____

_____

_____

MARCH 2:

(F) Romans 1:17 (For in it the righteousness of God is revealed from faith to faith, as it says, "The righteous shall live by faith.") We have no separation from God. God has declared us worthy through our faith in Jesus Christ. So as "righteous ones," it is inevitable that we live by faith. Faith is how we unite with Christ.

- Broad application: Be one with Christ.
- Your application:

_____

_____

_____

_____

_____

_____

_____

_____

_____

_____

_____

_____

_____

_____

_____

_____

_____

_____

_____

MARCH 3:

(F) Hebrews 11:1 (Now faith is the substance of things hoped for, the evidence of things not seen.) Faith assures us that Jesus Christ will return for His people. And we can depend on that to come to pass. Faith also proves that we believe Jesus died for our sins and now intercedes with our Father on our behalf. Faith is hope for the future and evidence of the present.

- Broad application: Hope and confirm.
- Your application:

_____

_____

_____

_____

_____

_____

_____

_____

_____

_____

_____

_____

_____

_____

_____

_____

_____

_____

_____

MARCH 4:

(GE) Ephesians 4:32 (Be kind to one another, tenderhearted, forgiving one another, as God in Christ forgave you.) Examples of being unkind are in the previous verse. They involve bitterness, wrath, anger, and speaking bad words. As new beings in Christ, we put away these old desires. And we also learn to forgive the faults of others as Jesus forgave ours.

- Broad application: Be kind and forgiving.
- Your application:

_____

_____

_____

_____

_____

_____

_____

_____

_____

_____

_____

_____

_____

_____

_____

_____

_____

_____

_____

MARCH 5:

(GO) Matthew 5:15-16 ("Neither do people light a lamp and put it under a basket. Instead, they put it on its stand, giving everyone in the house light. In the same way, let your light shine before others so that they may see your good works and give glory to your Father who is in heaven.") Our light should shine before others. And not in a boastful way, but as an example. Our good behavior should reflect the God we serve so others will want to know Him. These acts glorify God. He is the light in this dark evil world.

- Broad application: Light up the world.
- Your application:

_____

_____

_____

_____

_____

_____

_____

_____

_____

_____

_____

_____

_____

_____

_____

_____

_____

MARCH 6:

(J) 2 Corinthians 9:7 (Each one must give as he has decided in his heart, not reluctantly or under compulsion, for God loves a cheerful giver.) We are required to help those in need. But when we do, we should do it willingly. We know who blesses us and how part of that blessing is to bless others. As Christians, that should give us great joy.

- Broad application: Have joy in giving.
- Your application:

_____
_____
_____
_____
_____
_____
_____
_____
_____
_____
_____
_____
_____
_____
_____
_____
_____
_____
_____

MARCH 7:

(LS) Galatians 6:2 (Bear each other's burdens, and so fulfill the law of Christ.) Christians should certainly be concerned about each other's spiritual walk. We should be there to guide and encourage each other patiently. We should want to be the instruments used to carry out the will of our Father. Bearing one another's burdens should be a privilege.

- Broad application: Lean on me.
- Your application:

_____

_____

_____

_____

_____

_____

_____

_____

_____

_____

_____

_____

_____

_____

_____

_____

_____

_____

_____

_____

March 8:

(L) 1 John 4:12 (No one has ever seen God; if we love one another, God abides in us, and his love gets perfected in us.) No one has ever laid eyes on our Father. But we still know his characteristics. He lives in us. So when we show love to others, He is seen as perfection!

- Broad application: See me. See God.
- Your application:

_____
_____
_____
_____
_____
_____
_____
_____
_____
_____
_____
_____
_____
_____
_____
_____
_____
_____

MARCH 9:

(M) Proverbs 15:33 (The fear of the Lord is an instruction in wisdom, and humility comes before honor.) We should be in awe of our Creator and fear His wrath. It is wise to do so. It is also wise to humble ourselves. No one loves or respects anyone who is conceited.

- Broad application: Be wise and humble.
- Your application:

_____

_____

_____

_____

_____

_____

_____

_____

_____

_____

_____

_____

_____

_____

_____

_____

_____

_____

_____

MARCH 10:

(P) Numbers 6:26 (The Lord lifts his countenance upon you and gives you peace.) Christians have a powerful backer. When we have God's endorsement, nothing the world throws at us can stop us. We know He approves of us and is there to help us in our time of need. Knowing this gives us total peace.

- Broad application: Count on His support.
- Your application:

_____
_____
_____
_____
_____
_____
_____
_____
_____
_____
_____
_____
_____
_____
_____
_____
_____
_____
_____

MARCH 11:

(T) 1 Peter 5:8 (Be sober-minded; be watchful. Your adversary, the devil, prowls around like a roaring lion, seeking someone to devour.) Satan is not our friend. We must always be alert. His goal is to lead us away from the Lord and destroy our chance of salvation. We can not be intoxicated by what this world has to offer.

- Broad application: Dodge the devil.
- Your application:

_____

_____

_____

_____

_____

_____

_____

_____

_____

_____

_____

_____

_____

_____

_____

_____

_____

_____

_____

MARCH 12:

(F) Romans 10:10 (For with the heart one believes and is justified, and with the mouth, one confesses and has salvation.) We are righteous when we believe God raised Jesus from the dead. When we confess with our mouths Jesus as our Savior, God's grace leads us to salvation. Righteousness is by faith. Salvation is by faith.

- Broad application: Believe and confess.
- Your application:

_____

_____

_____

_____

_____

_____

_____

_____

_____

_____

_____

_____

_____

_____

_____

_____

_____

_____

_____

_____

MARCH 13:

(F) John 6:35 (Jesus said to them, "I am the bread of life; whoever comes to me shall not hunger, and whoever believes in me shall never thirst.") Jesus is the bread from heaven given to us by God. His spiritual food and water sustain us. We will never go hungry or thirsty. Through faith in Him, we will gain eternal life.

- Broad application: Eat from Jesus's table.
- Your application:

_____
_____
_____
_____
_____
_____
_____
_____
_____
_____
_____
_____
_____
_____
_____
_____
_____
_____
_____

MARCH 14:

(GE) Ephesians 4:1-2 (I, therefore, a prisoner for the Lord, urge that you walk worthy of the calling, with all humility and gentleness, with patience, bearing with one another in love.) As Paul, we should be proud to be prisoners for the Lord. We should be delighted to be "kept" by Him. We should be worthy of the position that His grace has given us. Therefore, we should practice humility, kindness, patience, and love as we share the Word with others. We have a critical job to do.

- Broad application: Walk in a kind manner.
- Your application:

_____

_____

_____

_____

_____

_____

_____

_____

_____

_____

_____

_____

_____

_____

_____

_____

_____

_____

MARCH 15:

(GO) 1 Timothy 2:9-10 (Likewise, women should adorn themselves in respectable apparel, with modesty and self-control, not with braided hair and gold or pearls or costly attire, but with what is proper for women who profess godliness—with good works.) As women, we desire to look good. God knows this; we are His design. But as Godly women, what is pleasing to the Lord comes first. We don't want our looks to take away from our good works. After all, <u>He</u> always looks good on us.

- Broad application: Let modesty be your testimony.
- Your application:

_____

_____

_____

_____

_____

_____

_____

_____

_____

_____

_____

_____

_____

_____

_____

_____

_____

_____

MARCH 16:

(J) Psalm 119:111 (Your testimonies are my heritage forever, for they are the joy of my heart.) God's Word is here for those of us who follow Him. We hand it down to our children and them to their children. It is a joy to bear witness to His promises. We rejoice in our rich heritage forever.

- Broad application: Testify!
- Your application:

_____
_____
_____
_____
_____
_____
_____
_____
_____
_____
_____
_____
_____
_____
_____
_____
_____
_____
_____

MARCH 17:

(LS) Isaiah 43:2 (When you pass through the waters, I will be with you; and through the rivers, they shall not overwhelm you; when you walk through fire you shall not be burned, and the flame shall not consume you.) God chooses us. He is our Redeemer. No trials can harm us because God is always by our side. He is our Savior and our salvation!

- Broad application: Know He is near.
- Your application:

_____

_____

_____

_____

_____

_____

_____

_____

_____

_____

_____

_____

_____

_____

_____

_____

_____

_____

_____

MARCH 18:

(L) 1 Corinthians 13:2 (If I have prophetic powers, understand all mysteries and knowledge, and have all faith to remove mountains, but I don't have love, I am nothing.) God has given all of us specific gifts or parts to play. But none are more important than the ability to love one another. The body of Christ (the church) cannot function without it. Love is the only thing that never fails.

- Broad application: Play the love role.
- Your application:

_____

_____

_____

_____

_____

_____

_____

_____

_____

_____

_____

_____

_____

_____

_____

_____

_____

_____

MARCH 19:

(M) Galatians 5:13 (For God called you to freedom, brothers. Only do not use your freedom as an opportunity for the flesh, but through love serve one another.) Through Jesus Christ, we are free from the law. But being free does not mean we can do anything we want. It is a chance to show love. Being free means we can humble ourselves and serve others.

- Broad application: Feel free to serve.
- Your application:

_____

_____

_____

_____

_____

_____

_____

_____

_____

_____

_____

_____

_____

_____

_____

_____

_____

_____

_____

_____

MARCH 20:

(P) James 3:17 (But the wisdom from above is first pure, then peace-able, gentle, open to reason, full of mercy and good fruits, impartial and sincere.) To be wise requires a level of peace. Sound judgment is needed. When we are grounded in the Word of God, we tend to look for common ground. Common ground is peaceful.

- Broad application: Search for peace.
- Your application:

_____
_____
_____
_____
_____
_____
_____
_____
_____
_____
_____
_____
_____
_____
_____
_____
_____
_____
_____
_____

MARCH 21:

(T) Philippians 4:13 (I can do everything through him who strengthens me.) Each day has its challenges in the life of a Christian. But we live through them because Christ lives through us. He gives us the strength to adapt and adjust. Nothing is too big for Him.

- Broad application: Bank on His strength.
- Your application:

_____

_____

_____

_____

_____

_____

_____

_____

_____

_____

_____

_____

_____

_____

_____

_____

_____

_____

_____

MARCH 22:

(F) Psalm 119:30 (I have chosen the way of faithfulness; I set your rules before me.) The way to righteousness is a choice. When we follow Jesus Christ, we are on a particular path. His rules and guidelines become our rules and procedures. Our faith guides our actions.

- Broad application: Stay on His path.
- Your application:

_____

_____

_____

_____

_____

_____

_____

_____

_____

_____

_____

_____

_____

_____

_____

_____

_____

_____

_____

_____

MARCH 23:

(F) Mark 10:52 (And Jesus said to him, "Go your way; your faith has made you well." And immediately he recovered his sight and followed him on the way.) Sickness and medical conditions are a part of life. But when we find ourselves in those situations, we can pray to Jesus. He is still in the healing business. Our faith can see us through.

- Broad application: Believe in His power.
- Your application:

_____
_____
_____
_____
_____
_____
_____
_____
_____
_____
_____
_____
_____
_____
_____
_____
_____
_____
_____

MARCH 24:

(GE) 2 Timothy 2:24-25 (The Lord's servant must not be quarrelsome but kind to everyone, able to teach, patiently enduring evil, correcting his opponents with gentleness. God may grant them repentance leading to a knowledge of the truth.) We are soldiers in God's army. We should serve the Lord while avoiding bickering at all costs. We should be able to use patience and kindness when instructing others on His Word. He wants all of us to know Him, to know the truth. God wants all of us to repent and claim salvation.

- Broad application: Be kind when teaching others.
- Your application:

_____

_____

_____

_____

_____

_____

_____

_____

_____

_____

_____

_____

_____

_____

_____

_____

_____

March 25:

(GO) Jeremiah 29:11-12 (For I know the plans I have for you, declares the Lord, plans for welfare and not for evil, to give you a future and hope. Then you will call upon me and come and pray to me, and I will hear you.) These verses recall the phrase, "It's all good!" No matter what happens in life, God wants us to have a future and to have hope! He wants nothing but good things for His chosen people. Then we will forever be in His presence. Then we will call out to Him, and he will hear our prayers.

- Broad application: Seek God's good plan.
- Your application:

_____

_____

_____

_____

_____

_____

_____

_____

_____

_____

_____

_____

_____

_____

_____

_____

_____

_____

_____

MARCH 26:

(J) 1 Timothy 6:6 (But godliness with contentment is significant gain.) In today's world, losing sight of what's essential is easy. Nothing should come between our relationship with God. As we strive to be more Christ-like, we learn to be content with life's necessities, even though He blesses us above and beyond that. We find joy in knowing God is enough, and He will supply our every need.

- Broad application: Find joy in simplicity.
- Your application:

_____
_____
_____
_____
_____
_____
_____
_____
_____
_____
_____
_____
_____
_____
_____
_____
_____
_____

MARCH 27:

(LS) 2 Peter 3:9 (The Lord is not slow to fulfill his promise as some count slowness, but is patient toward you, not wishing that any should perish, but that all should reach repentance.) The Lord is coming back again. He does not lie. He is just too loving and patient beyond what any of us deserve. He wants none of us to miss the opportunity to repent and be saved.

- Broad application: Have God-like patience.
- Your application:

_____

_____

_____

_____

_____

_____

_____

_____

_____

_____

_____

_____

_____

_____

_____

_____

_____

_____

_____

MARCH 28:

(L) John 14:15 ("If you love me, you will keep my commandments.")
Love truly is an action word. There is behavior linked to this emotion.
The Holy Spirit guides us in the right direction. We strive to do the will
of our Father.

- Broad application: Let love lead me.
- Your application:

_____

_____

_____

_____

_____

_____

_____

_____

_____

_____

_____

_____

_____

_____

_____

_____

_____

_____

_____

_____

MARCH 29:

(M) Matthew 5:5 ("Blessed are the meek, for they shall inherit the earth.") Those who are meek (submissive) will be blessed. God likes it when we comply with His will. We can not be in the presence of God or serve Him without this characteristic. In doing so, our reward is here on earth and in heaven.

- Broad application: Be humble; be blessed.
- Your application:

_____
_____
_____
_____
_____
_____
_____
_____
_____
_____
_____
_____
_____
_____
_____
_____
_____
_____
_____
_____

MARCH 30:

(P) Romans 8:6 (For to set the mind on the flesh is death, but to set the mind on the Spirit is life and peace.) When we put our minds on worldly things, we refuse to submit to the will of God. What comes of this way of life is death and destruction. When we set our minds on the Spirit, there is life and peace. The Holy Spirit guarantees this.

- Broad application: Live by the Spirit.
- Your application:

_____

_____

_____

_____

_____

_____

_____

_____

_____

_____

_____

_____

_____

_____

_____

_____

_____

_____

_____

_____

March 31:

(T) Romans 8:13 (For if you live according to the flesh you will die, but if by the Spirit you put to death the deeds of the body, you will live.) If we live according to what pleases us, it can only lead to death. But a life filled with the Holy Spirit leads to salvation. Through the Holy Spirit, we become more and more separated from the evil nature of the flesh. Deeds of the Spirit rule.

- Broad application: Deny the flesh.
- Your application:

_____

_____

_____

_____

_____

_____

_____

_____

_____

_____

_____

_____

_____

_____

_____

_____

_____

_____

APRIL 1:

(F) James 1:6 (But let him ask in faith, with no doubting, for the ones who doubt is like a wave of the sea that is driven and tossed by the wind.) When we pray to God, we should make our petitions known with unwavering faith. We should be confident in our Father's ability to meet our needs. We should be firm in our conviction. We should ask with certainty.

- Broad application: Expect things to happen.
- Your application:

_____

_____

_____

_____

_____

_____

_____

_____

_____

_____

_____

_____

_____

_____

_____

_____

_____

_____

APRIL 2:

(F) John 11:25-26 (Jesus said to her, "I am the resurrection and the life." Whoever believes in me, though he dies, yet shall he live, and everyone who lives and believes in me shall never die. Do you think this?") Lazarus had died and was in his tomb. Jesus is talking to Lazarus's sister Martha. He tells her that He holds the power of life and death in His hands. All that is needed Is faith in this. Do you believe it?

- Broad application: Hope for life.
- Your application:

_____

_____

_____

_____

_____

_____

_____

_____

_____

_____

_____

_____

_____

_____

_____

_____

_____

_____

APRIL 3:

(GE) Titus 3:3-4 (For we were once foolish, disobedient, led astray, enslaved to various passions and pleasures, passing our days in malice and envy, hated by others and hating one another. But when the goodness and loving kindness of God our Savior appeared...) Let us never forget that we were once willfully foolish and disobedient. We were easily influenced and followed all kinds of lusts and pleasures. Hatred and resentment were emotions some of us acted upon daily. But everything changed when God showered us with His grace and mercy, love, and kindness. We became new creatures.

- Broad application: Remember who you were.
- Your application:

_____

_____

_____

_____

_____

_____

_____

_____

_____

_____

_____

_____

_____

_____

_____

_____

APRIL 4:

(GO) Psalm 31:19-20 (Oh, how abundant are the good things that you have stored up for those who fear you, that you bestow in the sight of all, on those who take refuge in you. In the cover of your presence, you hide them from the plots of men; you store them in your shelter from the strife of tongues.) God has plenty of goodness for those who fear Him and take refuge in Him. The world sees His goodness toward us. He protects us from the evils of men. Schemes to destroy us will not prevail. Lies and deceit will not harm us.

- Broad application: Be in line for goodness.
- Your application:

_____
_____
_____
_____
_____
_____
_____
_____
_____
_____
_____
_____
_____
_____
_____
_____
_____

APRIL 5:

(J) 1 Timothy 6:17 (As for the rich in this present age, charge them not to be haughty, nor to set their hopes on the uncertainty of riches, but on God, who richly provides us with everything to enjoy.) If we are abundantly blessed financially, it is not the time to look down on those who are not. It is also not the time to rely on those riches to give us joy. Our joy still comes from the Lord. He alone holds the key to life's riches.

- Broad application: Search for genuine gold.
- Your application:

_____

_____

_____

_____

_____

_____

_____

_____

_____

_____

_____

_____

_____

_____

_____

_____

_____

_____

APRIL 6:

(LS) Hebrews 4:15 (For we do not have a high priest who is unable to sympathize with our weaknesses, but one who in every aspect has known temptation as we do yet is without sin.) Jesus came into this sin-filled world as flesh. He gave up His heavenly seat by our Father to do this. We are so blessed to have a Savior who knows what we go through but still has no sin. His grace and mercy will see us through.

- Broad application: Remember Jesus's journey.
- Your application:

_____
_____
_____
_____
_____
_____
_____
_____
_____
_____
_____
_____
_____
_____
_____
_____
_____
_____

APRIL 7:

(M) Proverbs 14:29 (Whoever is slow to anger has great understanding, but he who has a hasty temper exalts folly.) When we are slow to anger, we can give ourselves time to think before we act. We can use that time to assess the situation. But when we think or move too quickly, we promote foolishness. Humility shows us God's wisdom.

- Broad application: Stop and think.
- Your application:

_____

_____

_____

_____

_____

_____

_____

_____

_____

_____

_____

_____

_____

_____

_____

_____

_____

_____

_____

_____

April 8:

(P) Psalm 4:8 (In peace I will lie down and sleep; for you alone, O Lord, make me dwell in safety.) It is a privilege to go to the one who holds all things in His hands. What a blessing it is to find safety in His arms. We can have peaceful rest. We can enjoy a peaceful sleep.

- Broad application: Sleep peacefully.
- Your application:

_____

_____

_____

_____

_____

_____

_____

_____

_____

_____

_____

_____

_____

_____

_____

_____

_____

_____

_____

_____

April 9:

(L) John 15:13 ("Greater love has no one than this, that someone lay down his life for his friends.") Jesus is our true friend. He showed how much He loved us when he laid down His life for us. He chose us. What a friend we have in Jesus!

- Broad application: Love like Jesus.
- Your application:

_____
_____
_____
_____
_____
_____
_____
_____
_____
_____
_____
_____
_____
_____
_____
_____
_____
_____
_____

APRIL 10:

(T) 1 John 2:16 (Lust of the flesh, desires of the eyes, and pride of life do not come from the Father, but the world.) We are tempted by what we see and want in this world. These desires have the potential to consume us. But as Christians know, this world is not our home. We are only here for a little while.

- Broad application: Get ready to relocate.
- Your application:

_____

_____

_____

_____

_____

_____

_____

_____

_____

_____

_____

_____

_____

_____

_____

_____

_____

_____

_____

_____

APRIL 11:

(F) Acts 8:36-37 (And as they went along the road, they came to some water, and the eunuch said, "See, here is water! What prevents me from being baptized?" And Philip said, "If you believe with all your heart, you may." And he replied, "I believe that Jesus Christ is the Son of God.") Nothing prevents us from accepting Jesus Christ as our personal Savior. He has paid the price and made salvation available to us all. All that is needed is faith. All we have to do is believe He is the Son of God, who came in the flesh, died for our sins, and rose from the dead. We then may be baptized to show an outward sign of an inward change.

- Broad application: Show your allegiance to Christ.
- Your application:

_____

_____

_____

_____

_____

_____

_____

_____

_____

_____

_____

_____

_____

_____

_____

APRIL 12:

(F) Ephesians 3:16-17 (That according to the riches of his glory he may grant you to be strengthened with power through his Spirit in your inner being, so that Christ may dwell in your hearts through faith-that you, being rooted and grounded in love...) Here Paul is acknowledging that God has everything we need. And he believes He is willing to give it. Paul is also praying that Jesus strengthens His followers with the power of the Holy Spirit. He is praying that their faith will let them know God's love for them through that power. God wants to rest in us just as we want to rest in Him.

- Broad application: Have enough faith to rest.
- Your application:

_____

_____

_____

_____

_____

_____

_____

_____

_____

_____

_____

_____

_____

_____

_____

APRIL 13:

(GE) Colossians 4:5-6 (Walk in wisdom toward outsiders, making the best use of the time. Let your speech always be gracious, seasoned with salt, so that you may know how you ought to answer each person.) As children of God, we should always be mindful of unbelievers. We should watch and be wise, looking for opportunities to witness. And when those opportunities arise, we should speak with kindness and compassion. We should also draw on God's wisdom to answer any questions the unsaved may have. Their salvation is at stake.

- Broad application: Use both wisdom and kindness.
- Your application:

_____

_____

_____

_____

_____

_____

_____

_____

_____

_____

_____

_____

_____

_____

_____

_____

_____

_____

APRIL 14:

(GO) Amos 5:14-15 (Seek good, and not evil, that you may live; so the Lord, the God of hosts, will be with you, as you have said. Hate evil, love good, and establish justice in the gate; it may be that the Lord, the God of hosts, will be gracious to the remnant of Joseph.) Seek good, not evil, and the Lord will be with you. Hate evil, love good, and be righteous. God will be good and forgiving to the remnant of Joseph. That is true today. We are that remnant.

- Broad application: Act like God's remnant.
- Your application:

_____

_____

_____

_____

_____

_____

_____

_____

_____

_____

_____

_____

_____

_____

_____

_____

_____

_____

April 15:

(J) Zephaniah 3:17 (The Lord your God is in your midst, a mighty one who will save; he will rejoice over you with gladness; he will quiet you by his love; he will rejoice over you with loud singing.) God wants none of us to be lost. His love for us is beyond comparison. His saving grace is available to us all. It brings Him great joy to know we are His people.

- Broad application: Feel His presence.
- Your application:

April 16:

(LS) Philippians 1:29 (For it has been granted to you that for the sake of Christ you should not only believe in him but also suffer for his sake.) No one wants to suffer or endure pain, physical or otherwise. But it is inevitable when we serve Christ. It is a privilege to believe in Him and persevere for His sake. It is proof of our salvation.

- Broad application: Suffer for the Lord.
- Your application:

_____

_____

_____

_____

_____

_____

_____

_____

_____

_____

_____

_____

_____

_____

_____

_____

_____

_____

_____

APRIL 17:

(L) Romans 13:8 (Owe no one anything, except to love each other, for the one who loves another has fulfilled the law.) We owe a debt. We can never pay the debt, but we owe it all the same. Love covers every commandment. So by showing God's love to one another, we are made righteous.

- Broad application: Pay it forward.
- Your application:

_____
_____
_____
_____
_____
_____
_____
_____
_____
_____
_____
_____
_____
_____
_____
_____
_____
_____
_____
_____

April 18:

(M) Proverbs 17:1 (Better is a dry morsel with quiet than a house full of feasting with strife.) We need to live in peace. Conflict and friction are not the way of the Lord. Discord is not good among God's people. Having very little yet at ease is far better than having an abundance and living in turmoil.

- Broad application: Seek to be meek.
- Your application:

_____

_____

_____

_____

_____

_____

_____

_____

_____

_____

_____

_____

_____

_____

_____

_____

_____

_____

_____

APRIL 19:

(P) Philippians 4:7 (And the peace of God, which surpasses all understanding, will guard your hearts and minds in Christ Jesus.) We can
not begin to understand the kind of peace we have access to in Jesus
Christ. But we rest assured that God can handle any problem we face.
We can live in perfect harmony. He will protect our hearts and minds.

- Broad application: Accept His peace.
- Your application:

_____

_____

_____

_____

_____

_____

_____

_____

_____

_____

_____

_____

_____

_____

_____

_____

_____

_____

_____

APRIL 20:

(T) Romans 13:14 (But put on the Lord Jesus Christ, and make no provision for the flesh, to gratify its desires.) Sometimes it may seem natural to satisfy the flesh. After all, we have a sinful nature. So we may tend to look for ways to fulfill our desires. But when we cover ourselves with the Holy Spirit, it becomes just as natural to look for ways to satisfy God.

- Broad application: Satisfy Christ.
- Your application:

_____
_____
_____
_____
_____
_____
_____
_____
_____
_____
_____
_____
_____
_____
_____
_____
_____
_____
_____
_____

APRIL 21:

(F) Galatians 3:26-27 (For in Christ Jesus you are all sons of God, through faith. For as many of you as were baptized into Christ have put on Christ.) We are all sons and daughters of God through faith in Jesus Christ. Before Him, we were under the law. The law pointed out our sins but offered no true deliverance from them. But now, being baptized into Christ, we see our transformation. Our faith in Him has set us free.

- Broad application: Be in God's family.
- Your application:

_____

_____

_____

_____

_____

_____

_____

_____

_____

_____

_____

_____

_____

_____

_____

_____

_____

_____

APRIL 22:

(F) Romans 4:20-21 (No unbelief made him waver concerning the promise of God, but he grew strong in his faith as he gave glory to God, fully convinced that God was able to do what he had promised.) God promised Abraham he would become the father of many nations. His faith in God's promise never wavered. It grew stronger! And as his belief grew, he gave God all the glory, honor, and praise He deserved. He did not doubt that God could do just what He said He would do.

- Broad application: Never waiver.
- Your application:

_____

_____

_____

_____

_____

_____

_____

_____

_____

_____

_____

_____

_____

_____

_____

_____

_____

_____

_____

APRIL 23:

(GE) Romans 15:6-7 (...that together you may with one voice glorify the God and Father of our Lord Jesus Christ. Therefore welcome one another as Christ has welcomed you, for the glory of God.) God's glory is magnified when we come together and exalt His name. But we cannot do this if we are not kind to one another. We cannot do this if we are not accepting of each other. We can, however, do this if we remember how Jesus was kind to us and how He received us. He also did this to glorify His Father.

- Broad application: Unite for God's glory.
- Your application:

_____

_____

_____

_____

_____

_____

_____

_____

_____

_____

_____

_____

_____

_____

_____

_____

_____

APRIL 24:

(GO) Psalm 23:5-6 (You prepare a table before me in the presence of my enemies; you anoint my head with oil; my cup overflows. Surely goodness and mercy shall follow me all the days of my life, and I shall dwell in the house of the Lord forever.) God still gives us what we need in the most trying circumstances. He also supplies us with the Holy Spirit. He gives us more than enough. His goodness is forever. We have a place with Him forever.

- Broad application: Prepare for God's goodness.
- Your application:

_____

_____

_____

_____

_____

_____

_____

_____

_____

_____

_____

_____

_____

_____

_____

_____

_____

APRIL 25:

(J) Romans 12:12 (Rejoice in hope, be patient in tribulation, be constant in prayer.) These are just a few reminders while serving the Lord. We should rejoice in the hope of His return. We need to be patient in times of uncertainty. We should always be in prayer.

- Broad application: Rejoice. Be patient. Pray.
- Your application:

_____

_____

_____

_____

_____

_____

_____

_____

_____

_____

_____

_____

_____

_____

_____

_____

_____

_____

April 26:

(LS) Romans 5:3-4 (We rejoice in our sufferings, knowing that suffering produces endurance, endurance produces character, and character produces hope.) We rejoice in our trials and tribulations here on earth. We know our pain and suffering help us to be patient and wait on the Lord. We also know that patience builds Christian character. It gives us the ability to hope. And that hope leads to salvation.

- Broad application: Understand the process.
- Your application:

_____
_____
_____
_____
_____
_____
_____
_____
_____
_____
_____
_____
_____
_____
_____
_____
_____
_____

APRIL 27:

(L) 1 John 3:1 (See what kind of love the Father has given to us, that He should call us His children; and so we are. The reason why the world does not know us is that it did not know him.) Our Father loves us, so we are called His children. The world does not acknowledge us because they did not acknowledge Him. But that is ok. We do not belong to the world.

- Broad application: Know not the world.
- Your application:

_____
_____
_____
_____
_____
_____
_____
_____
_____
_____
_____
_____
_____
_____
_____
_____
_____
_____
_____

April 28:

(M) Amos 3:3 (Do two walk together unless they have agreed to meet?) God has allowed us to be a part of His intended covenant with us through His Son, Jesus Christ. We can not walk in His will without it. But we must take an active role in this journey. We must agree to meet with Him.

- Broad application: Meet Him all way.
- Your application:

_____
_____
_____
_____
_____
_____
_____
_____
_____
_____
_____
_____
_____
_____
_____
_____
_____
_____
_____
_____

APRIL 29:

(P) John 14:27 ("Peace I leave with you; my peace I give to you. Not as the world gives to you. Let not your hearts be troubled, neither let them be afraid.") Jesus offers true peace and comfort to us. There is nothing else like it in the world. The world does not have it to give. Our worries and fears are washed away in His care.

- Broad application: Seek heavenly peace.
- Your application:

_____
_____
_____
_____
_____
_____
_____
_____
_____
_____
_____
_____
_____
_____
_____
_____
_____
_____
_____

April 30:

(T) Galatians 5:17 (The desires of the flesh are against the Spirit, and the wishes of the Spirit are against the flesh. These are opposed to each other to keep you from doing the things you want to do.) Lest we forget, we serve an omniscient God! He knows everything about His people. He has made it possible for us to keep the desires of our flesh in check through His unique Holy Spirit. When we rely on Him, we shall do His will.

- Broad application: Cease the struggle.
- Your application:

_____
_____
_____
_____
_____
_____
_____
_____
_____
_____
_____
_____
_____
_____
_____
_____
_____

MAY 1:

(F) Romans 8:24-25 (For in this hope we were saved. Now hope that we see is not hope. For who hopes for what he sees? But if we hope for what we do not know, we wait for it with patience.) Our salvation comes from faith in Jesus Christ. He is the only way. Our hope is not in someone we can see. Because who hopes for something they can see? Our hope helps us to wait for His return patiently.

- Broad application: Wait and see.
- Your application:

_____

_____

_____

_____

_____

_____

_____

_____

_____

_____

_____

_____

_____

_____

_____

_____

_____

_____

MAY 2:

(F) Matthew 21:21-22 (And Jesus answered them, "Truly, I say to you if you have faith and do not doubt, you will not only do what faith has done to the fig tree, but even if you say to this mountain, 'Be taken up and thrown into the sea,' it will happen. And whatever you ask in prayer, you will receive if you have faith.") Jesus had just commanded a fig tree not to bear any more fruit. It then immediately died. Here He is telling his disciples that if their faith never wavered, they could do the same. They could ask and speak anything into existence. Through dedication and prayer, miracles like this can happen.

- Broad application: Think big.
- Your application:

_____
_____
_____
_____
_____
_____
_____
_____
_____
_____
_____
_____
_____
_____
_____
_____

MAY 3:

(GE) Zechariah 7:9-10 (Thus says the Lord of hosts, Render true judgments, show kindness and mercy to one another, do not oppress the widow, the fatherless, the sojourner, or the poor, and let none of you devise evil against another in your heart.) The Lord says we should make moral decisions. And He instructs us on how to do so. He tells us we should be kind to those suffering or lost, such as widows, the fatherless, strangers, or the poor. We should show compassion. We should also never have hatred in our hearts to do evil or harm to anyone.

- Broad application: Have a kind heart.
- Your application:

_____

_____

_____

_____

_____

_____

_____

_____

_____

_____

_____

_____

_____

_____

_____

_____

MAY 4:

(G0) Philippians 4:8-9 (Finally brothers, whatever is true, whatever is honorable, whatever is just, whatever is pure, whatever is lovely, whatever is commendable, if there is any excellence, if there is anything worthy of praise, think about these things. What you have learned, received, heard, and seen in me- practice these things, and the God of peace will be with you.) We should focus on what is true, honest, and just. We should focus on what is pure, beautiful, and deserving. We should move our attention to all things that are of God. Emulate these virtues that you see in others. The peace of God will be with you.

- Broad application: Indulge in goodness.
- Your application:

_____
_____
_____
_____
_____
_____
_____
_____
_____
_____
_____
_____
_____
_____
_____
_____

May 5:

(J) Ecclesiastes 9:7 (Go, eat your bread with joy, and drink your wine with a merry heart, for God has already approved what you do.) One way the devil tries to discredit the Christian lifestyle is by perpetuating the myth that our lives are dull. He preys on the unsaved by telling them their good times are over. But here we see God is saying it is ok to have fun and be happy. A life with God as our Father is enjoyable.

- Broad application: Eat. Drink. Be merry.
- Your application:

_____

_____

_____

_____

_____

_____

_____

_____

_____

_____

_____

_____

_____

_____

_____

_____

_____

_____

MAY 6:

(LS) Hebrews 12:2-3 (We look to Jesus, the founder and perfecter of our faith. He willingly endured the cross, despite the shame, and is seated at the right hand of the throne of God. Consider him who endured from sinners such hostility against himself, so that you may not grow weary or fainthearted.) Jesus is the reason we have faith. He was happy to fulfill the will of our Father even though He endured such shame, ridicule, and hostility. But our Savior stayed the course. He now sits at the right hand of the throne of God. Jesus is our best example of endurance.

- Broad application: Follow the cross.
- Your application:

_____
_____
_____
_____
_____
_____
_____
_____
_____
_____
_____
_____
_____
_____
_____
_____

MAY 7:

(L) Romans 12:10 (Love one another with brotherly affection. Outdo one another in showing honor.) As we love our biological brothers and sisters, we should also love our spiritual brothers and sisters. It is an honor to show God's love to one another. When we honor each other with love, we also celebrate our Father. We should always be quick to love.

- Broad application: Race to love.
- Your application:

_____

_____

_____

_____

_____

_____

_____

_____

_____

_____

_____

_____

_____

_____

_____

_____

_____

_____

MAY 8:

(M) Zephaniah 3:11-12 (On that day you, Jerusalem, will not be put to shame for all the wrongs you have done to me because I will remove from you your arrogant boasters. Never again will you be haughty on my holy hill. But I will leave within you the meek and humble. The remnant of Israel will trust in the name of the Lord.) This promise is accurate and relevant today. It is prophecy. When Jesus returns for His people, He will remove the rebellious and proud. We will stand before Him, humble and restored. We will trust in the name of the Lord.

- Broad application: Look forward to that day.
- Your application:

_____

_____

_____

_____

_____

_____

_____

_____

_____

_____

_____

_____

_____

_____

_____

_____

MAY 9:

(P) Romans 15:13 (May the God of hope fill you with all joy and peace in believing, so that by the power of the Holy Spirit you may abound in hope.) God gives many gifts. Through the Holy Spirit, we have joy and peace. Our faith produces jubilation! When we have faith and hope in God, it can bring about an abundance of peace.

- Broad application: Peace be with you.
- Your application:

_____

_____

_____

_____

_____

_____

_____

_____

_____

_____

_____

_____

_____

_____

_____

_____

_____

_____

_____

MAY 10:

(T) 2 Timothy 1:7 (For God gave us a spirit not of fear but power, love and self-control.) The temptations and trials of life can be overwhelming at times. But we can face our appetites, emotions, and attitudes without fear. He has equipped us with power, love, and self-control through the Holy Spirit. We can stand with courage.

- Broad application: Reel fear in.
- Your application:

_____
_____
_____
_____
_____
_____
_____
_____
_____
_____
_____
_____
_____
_____
_____
_____
_____
_____
_____
_____

MAY 11:

(F) John 8:23-24 (He said to them, "You are from below; I am from above. You are of this world; I am not of this world. I told you that you would die in your sins, for unless you believe I am he, you will die in your sins.") We live here on earth and are of this world. Jesus came from above to be in the flesh and live among us here on earth. He was not of this world. While here on earth, he died for our sins, yet rose again. Faith in this has, is, and will forever be our only way to salvation.

- Broad application: Believe in the resurrection.
- Your application:

_____
_____
_____
_____
_____
_____
_____
_____
_____
_____
_____
_____
_____
_____
_____
_____

MAY 12:

(F) James 2:17-18 (So faith by itself, if it does not have works, is dead. But someone will say, "You have faith and I have works." Show me your faith apart from your works, and I will show you my faith by my works.) Faith and works go hand in hand. Faith is both a noun and a verb. Each individual has both, not one or the other. If you possess the noun faith, you own the verb faith. It is impossible to believe in God and not do His will on His behalf.

- Broad application: Let your faith work.
- Your application:

_____
_____
_____
_____
_____
_____
_____
_____
_____
_____
_____
_____
_____
_____
_____
_____
_____
_____

MAY 13:

(GO) Luke 18:18-19 (And a ruler asked him, "Good Teacher, what must I do to inherit eternal life?" And Jesus said to him, "Why do you call me good? No one is good except God alone.") Jesus was asked a question by a young ruler who addressed Him as "Good Teacher." Jesus wanted to address this issue first. He wanted the young man to know there was no one good except God the Father. Everyone should know He was sent by the "Good One. It was because of His Father's goodness that man would become righteous.

- Broad application: Remember God, the "Good one."
- Your application:

_____

_____

_____

_____

_____

_____

_____

_____

_____

_____

_____

_____

_____

_____

_____

_____

_____

_____

MAY 14:

(GE) Proverbs 31:26 (She opens her mouth with wisdom, and the teaching of kindness is on her tongue.) Although this verse talks about a woman demonstrating knowledge in the home, we know that all need God's wisdom. All of us can have Godly wisdom if we seek it. We can speak with understanding. It can teach us to be kind.

- Broad application: Follow her lead.
- Your application:

_____

_____

_____

_____

_____

_____

_____

_____

_____

_____

_____

_____

_____

_____

_____

_____

_____

_____

_____

MAY 15:

(J) Psalm 30:5 (For his anger is but for a moment, and his favor is for a lifetime. Weeping may tarry for the night, but joy comes with the morning.) God's wrath is just for a moment because his desire is for us to have eternal life. The pain and sorrow we experience in this life are also fleeting. They may seem dark and looming at the time but hold on. God will give us a brighter day full of His renewed grace and mercy.

- Broad application: Ride the tide.
- Your application:

_____
_____
_____
_____
_____
_____
_____
_____
_____
_____
_____
_____
_____
_____
_____
_____
_____
_____

MAY 16:

(LS) 1 Peter 4:12-13 (Beloved, do not be surprised at the fiery trial when it comes upon you to test you, as though something strange was happening to you. But rejoice insofar as you share Christ's sufferings, that you may also rejoice and be glad when his glory reveals itself.) As ambassadors of Christ, we should not be surprised to know the suffering we must endure and the sacrifices we must make. We should rejoice in it. Jesus suffered on our behalf to fulfill the law and to save our souls. We will also have tests as we spread the "Good News" about our Lord and Savior, Jesus Christ. It is all for the glory of God.

- Broad application: Share in His trials.
- Your application:

MAY 17:

(L) Romans 5:8 (But God shows his love for us in that while we were still sinners, Christ died for us.) God did not wait for us to "get right." Time and time again, we proved we were not up for that challenge. He sent Jesus to die for us while we were still sinners. That kind of love is rare.

- Broad application: Love regardless.
- Your application:

_____

_____

_____

_____

_____

_____

_____

_____

_____

_____

_____

_____

_____

_____

_____

_____

_____

_____

_____

_____

MAY 18:

(M) Psalm 34:5-6 (Those who look to him are radiant, and their faces shall never be ashamed. This poor man cried, and the Lord heard him and saved him from all his troubles.) When we cry out to the Lord, we beam with His Spirit. We know we are redeemed and delivered. The past is the past. We are no longer ashamed. We are made humble in His presence.

- Broad application: Humble yourself to shine.
- Your application:

_____
_____
_____
_____
_____
_____
_____
_____
_____
_____
_____
_____
_____
_____
_____
_____
_____
_____
_____

MAY 19:

(P) Romans 5:1-2 (Therefore, since we are justified by faith, we have peace with God through our Lord Jesus Christ. Through faith in Jesus, we also have access to his grace. We will stand on the promise of grace and rejoice in the hope of the glory of God.) Because of our faith in God, we are righteous through our Lord and Savior, Jesus Christ. We can be at peace. We are no longer at odds with our maker. And through Jesus Christ, we also have access to that faith and can come before our Father anytime. We can rejoice because we know God's grace is all we need for salvation.

- Broad application: Expect peaceful joy.
- Your application:

_____

_____

_____

_____

_____

_____

_____

_____

_____

_____

_____

_____

_____

_____

_____

_____

MAY 20:

(T) Luke 21:34 ("Be careful not to be weighed down with carousing, drunkenness, and the anxieties of life, because that day will close on you suddenly like a trap.") As Christians, we are still not exempt from the temptations of this world. That is why we must watch for things that may permanently harm our general well-being and separate us from God forever. We must always be vigilant. We should always find time to be in prayer, the Word, and the Spirit.

- Broad application: Watch out.
- Your application:

_____
_____
_____
_____
_____
_____
_____
_____
_____
_____
_____
_____
_____
_____
_____
_____
_____
_____
_____

MAY 21:

(F) 1 Timothy 6:9-10 (But those who desire to be rich fall into temptation, into a snare, into many senseless and harmful desires that plunge people into ruin and destruction. For the love of money is the root of all kinds of evil. Through this craving, some have wandered away from the faith and pierced themselves with many pangs.) When one makes it their goal to be rich, it opens the door to many foolish and dangerous things that may lead to death and destruction. The love of money can be the source of all kinds of evil. And because of this lost love, a person may put aside their faith in God. They lose focus on what is essential. Their days become full of unnecessary misery and suffering.

- Broad application: Put nothing before God.
- Your application:

_____

_____

_____

_____

_____

_____

_____

_____

_____

_____

_____

_____

_____

_____

_____

MAY 22:

(F) John 6:28-29 (Then they said to him, "What must we do to be doing the works of God?" Jesus answered them, "This is the work of God, that you believe in him whom he has sent.") There are good people who do good things. It is part of who they are, and we should commend them for doing so. And some may consider their works to be for the Lord. But the Word is clear on this. God's work begins when we first believe He sent His son Jesus to redeem us.

- Broad application: Know your Master.
- Your application:

_____

_____

_____

_____

_____

_____

_____

_____

_____

_____

_____

_____

_____

_____

_____

_____

_____

May 23:

(GE) Proverbs 15:3-4 (The eyes of the Lord are in every place, keeping watch on the evil and the good. A gentle tongue is a tree of life, but perverseness in it breaks the spirit.) We know God can see everything because He is everywhere (omnipresent). He sees the good and the bad. So God sees and hears how we talk to others. Kind words have the power to comfort and heal. But evil words can corrupt the spirit.

- Broad application: Use healing words.
- Your application:

_____

_____

_____

_____

_____

_____

_____

_____

_____

_____

_____

_____

_____

_____

_____

_____

_____

_____

_____

MAY 24:

(GO) Galatians 6:8-9 (For the one who sows to his flesh will from the flesh reap corruption, but the one who sows to the Spirit will from the Spirit reap eternal life. And let us not grow weary of doing good, for in due season we will reap, if we do not give up.) The Word of God says we will reap what we sow. So if the flesh leads us, we will reap destruction. If the Spirit leads us, we will reap eternal life. And as we walk in the Spirit, we will be compelled to do good deeds. And we will not get tired of doing good because we know it will pay off in the end.

- Broad application: Stick around for the benefits.
- Your application:

_____

_____

_____

_____

_____

_____

_____

_____

_____

_____

_____

_____

_____

_____

_____

_____

_____

_____

MAY 25:

(J) Philippians 3:1-2 (Finally, my brothers, rejoice in the Lord. To write the same things to you is no trouble to me and is safe for you. Look out for the dogs, look out for the evildoers, look out for those who mutilate the flesh.) Paul tells the Philippians to rejoice in the Lord. He reminds them to stay focused on their faith in Jesus Christ, the only thing that leads to salvation. The Jews were telling them they needed circumcision for salvation. Paul warned them to look out for those who said they were unworthy of God's love just because they didn't follow certain rituals. Rejoice in knowing the Lord!

- Broad application: Know whom you serve.
- Your application:

_____

_____

_____

_____

_____

_____

_____

_____

_____

_____

_____

_____

_____

_____

_____

MAY 26:

(LS) 2 Corinthians 4:8-9 (We have hardships at every turn, but not crushed; perplexed, but not driven to despair; persecuted, but not forsaken; struck down, but not destroyed.) When we live for Christ, there can be trouble all around us, yet we will not crumble. We can be puzzled yet still have hope. We can suffer abuse yet not go through it alone. We can have setbacks yet come out on top. We will survive because we know a God who is able!

- Broad application: Accept some battle scars.
- Your application:

_____

_____

_____

_____

_____

_____

_____

_____

_____

_____

_____

_____

_____

_____

_____

_____

_____

_____

MAY 27:

(L) Psalm 143:8 (Let me hear in the morning of your steadfast love, for in you I trust. Make me know the way I should go, for to you I lift my soul.) It is essential to experience love. And those people we love are the ones we tend to trust the most. So when we love God, we look to Him for guidance. We put our lives in His hands.

- Broad application: In God we trust.
- Your application:

_____

_____

_____

_____

_____

_____

_____

_____

_____

_____

_____

_____

_____

_____

_____

_____

_____

_____

_____

_____

MAY 28:

(M) Philippians 2:14-15 (Do all things without grumbling or disputing, that you may be blameless and innocent, children of God without blemish in a crooked and twisted generation, among whom you shine as lights in the world.) God does not want us quarreling among ourselves. He wants us focused and united for His sake. We must remember that we are on a mission. And that mission puts us in the middle of a dark and lost world. His light cannot shine through us if our souls are dim.

- Broad application: Humble yourself for His cause.
- Your application:

_____
_____
_____
_____
_____
_____
_____
_____
_____
_____
_____
_____
_____
_____
_____
_____
_____
_____
_____

MAY 29:

(P) 1 Peter 3:10-11 (For "Whoever desires to love life and see good days, let him keep his tongue from evil and his lips from speaking deceit; turn away from sin and do good; seek peace and pursue it.") We are in line to inherit blessings when we serve the Lord. And those blessings are waiting for us here on earth. So if we want to love life and enjoy it, we must learn not to lie or twist the truth. We must not do evil for evil. We should follow these instructions to have God's blessings of favor and peace.

- Broad application: Have favor and peace.
- Your application:

_____

_____

_____

_____

_____

_____

_____

_____

_____

_____

_____

_____

_____

_____

_____

_____

MAY 30:

(T) Isaiah 5:22 (Woe to those who are heroes at drinking wine, and valiant men in mixing strong drink.) The Bible is full of warnings against excessive drinking. God knows what is not suitable for His creation. He knows how mind-altering chemicals can impair our thoughts and influence our actions. We must heed His warnings.

- Broad application: Stay sober.
- Your application:

_____

_____

_____

_____

_____

_____

_____

_____

_____

_____

_____

_____

_____

_____

_____

_____

_____

_____

_____

_____

MAY 31:

(F) Romans 1:15-16 (So I am eager to preach the gospel to you also who are in Rome. I am not ashamed of the gospel, for it is the power of God for salvation to everyone who believes, to the Jew first and also to the Greek.) Paul was eager and unashamed to preach the gospel. We should be just as enthusiastic and shameless, no matter how sophisticated or educated our audience may seem. The Word of God is the power of God. Jesus's death, burial, and resurrection are the basis of our faith. And that faith has the power to save anyone.

- Broad application: Proudly preach the Word.
- Your application:

_____

_____

_____

_____

_____

_____

_____

_____

_____

_____

_____

_____

_____

_____

_____

_____

_____

JUNE 1:

(F) Galatians 5:5-6 (For through the Spirit, by faith, we eagerly wait for the hope of righteousness. For in Christ Jesus, neither circumcision nor uncircumcision counts for anything, but only faith working through love.) We rely on the Holy Spirit to strengthen our faith. In turn, that faith gives us hope for salvation. We do not trust our salvation to rituals such as circumcision. The confidence we have comes from God's love for us. Our faith produces Godly love.

- Broad application: Be about faith and love.
- Your application:

JUNE 2:

(GE) Romans 14:12-13 (So each of us will give an account of himself to God. Therefore let us not pass judgment on one another any longer but rather decide never to put a stumbling block or hindrance in the way of a brother.) We will all give an account of our deeds to God. He will judge, not man. So we can save our futile judgments of one another. Our focus should be on making it a point not to hinder anyone's journey here on earth. We should be kind enough not to contribute to our brother's downfall by exhibiting immoral behavior that is offensive or imitated.

- Broad application: Watch your step.
- Your application:

_____

_____

_____

_____

_____

_____

_____

_____

_____

_____

_____

_____

_____

_____

_____

June 3:

(GO) 2 Timothy 3:16-17 (God breathes out all scripture, and it is profitable for teaching, reproof, correction, and training in righteousness, that the man of God may be complete, equipped for every good work.) God inspires His Word. His Word teaches us what is right and wrong and how to correct what is wrong. It shows us how to live a righteous life. It is all the instructions we need. When we apply it to our lives, we can do good works for the Lord.

- Broad application: Know what is good.
- Your application:

_____
_____
_____
_____
_____
_____
_____
_____
_____
_____
_____
_____
_____
_____
_____
_____
_____
_____

JUNE 4:

(J) Habakkuk 3:17-18 (Though the fig tree should not blossom, nor fruit be on the vines, the produce of the olive oil fail and the fields yield no food, the flock escapes the fold and there be no herd in the stalls, yet I will rejoice in the Lord; I will take joy in the God of my salvation.) I will rejoice if there isn't any fruit on the trees or vines. If there isn't any oil or food, I will rejoice. If there isn't any livestock in the barn, I will rejoice. I will rejoice in knowing the Lord. I will rejoice in my salvation.

- Broad application: Always rejoice in Him.
- Your application:

_____

_____

_____

_____

_____

_____

_____

_____

_____

_____

_____

_____

_____

_____

_____

_____

_____

_____

JUNE 5:

(LS) 1 Peter 1:6-7 (Even though we may have grieved through many trials, we will rejoice in the end. We will rejoice because our problems were necessary to test our faith which is more precious than gold. We want to give Jesus all the praise, honor, and glory as he reveals himself to us.) We should be glad when we go through trials and tribulations. Through them, our faith becomes more robust. Life's circumstances allow us to draw nearer to Jesus and rely on His Word. And as we trust in Him, we further see who He is. That revelation enables us to give Him all the glory, honor, and praise He so richly deserves.

- Broad application: Be able to stand.
- Your application:

_____
_____
_____
_____
_____
_____
_____
_____
_____
_____
_____
_____
_____
_____
_____
_____
_____

JUNE 6:

(L) 1 John 4:7 (Beloved, let us love one another, for love is from God, and whoever loves has been born of God and knows God.) True love is from God. That is why He sent His Son because He loves us that much. That kind of love is what we should have for each other. It is sent from God when we know who God is.

- Broad application: Know God's love.
- Your application:

_____

_____

_____

_____

_____

_____

_____

_____

_____

_____

_____

_____

_____

_____

_____

_____

_____

_____

_____

_____

_____

JUNE 7:

(M) Zephaniah 2:2-3 (...before the decree takes effect and that day passes like windblown chaff, before the Lord's fierce anger comes upon you, before the day of the Lord's wrath comes upon you. Seek the Lord, all you humble of the land, who do his just commands; seek righteousness; seek humility; perhaps God may hide you on the day of the anger of the Lord.) Our God has infinite patience, but His Word promises a day of judgment. So before that day comes, we should seek Him. We should humble ourselves and follow His commandments. We should submit to His will as His desires become our desires. Then, and only then, are we saved from His wrath.

- Broad application: Be humble to the end.
- Your application:

_____
_____
_____
_____
_____
_____
_____
_____
_____
_____
_____
_____
_____
_____
_____
_____
_____

JUNE 8:

(P) Romans 14:17-18 (For the kingdom of God is not a matter of eating and drinking but of righteousness and peace and joy in the Holy Spirit. Whoever thus serves Christ is acceptable to God and approved by men.) Here, Paul refers to food and drinks used in pagan rituals or things people once restricted under the law. Either way, he is warning believers not to get caught up in things that are of no concern to God. God is always concerned about the Holy Spirit's righteousness, peace, and joy. But when we "nitpick" about things that are not sinful in themselves, we cause discord among ourselves and in the church. We are acceptable to God if we serve Christ, and men should also approve.

- Broad application: Don't sweat the small stuff.
- Your application:

_____

_____

_____

_____

_____

_____

_____

_____

_____

_____

_____

_____

_____

_____

JUNE 9:

(T) 1 Corinthians 6:18-19 (Flee from sexual immorality. Every other sin a person commits is outside the body, but the sexually immoral person sins against his own body. Or do you not know that your body is a temple of the Holy Spirit within you, whom you have from God? You are not your own.) The Bible tells us to flee from sexual immorality. Escaping is the only assurance we have for restraint. Every other sin is outside the body, but the person who is sexually immoral sins within. And when we do this, we sin against the place where the Holy Spirit (Jesus) resides. As Christians, we are one with Him.

- Broad application: Remember to whom you belong.
- Your application:

_____
_____
_____
_____
_____
_____
_____
_____
_____
_____
_____
_____
_____
_____
_____
_____

JUNE 10:

(F) Hebrews 3:12-13 (Take care, brothers, lest there be evil, unbelieving hearts in any of you, leading you to fall away from the living God. But exhort one another every day, as long as it is "today," that none of you may grow hardened by the deceitfulness of sin.) We should all be cautious not to be tempted or persuaded to fall away from the true and living God. Temptation can indeed happen through the evil works of the devil. We should cling to our faith and trust in Jesus Christ. We can do this by encouraging one another daily. We can strengthen each other with the Word of God.

- Broad application: Encourage with the Truth.
- Your application:

_____

_____

_____

_____

_____

_____

_____

_____

_____

_____

_____

_____

_____

_____

_____

_____

JUNE 11:

(F) John 14:11-12 ("Believe me that I am in the Father and the Father is in me, or else believe on account of the works themselves. Truly, truly, I say to you, whoever believes in me will also do the deeds that I do, and more significant works than these will he do because I am going to the Father.") Before Jesus went to the cross, He tried to prepare His disciples for what was coming. He stressed that He was in the Father, and the Father was in Him. Or if they still were having a hard time with that concept, they could certainly believe in the works and miracles He had performed in His Father's name. Jesus wanted to assure them that His ministry would go on no matter what. He wanted them to believe they could do even greater works because they would have unlimited access to the Father through Him.

- Broad application: Tap into His greatness.
- Your application:

_____

_____

_____

_____

_____

_____

_____

_____

_____

_____

_____

_____

_____

JUNE 12:

(GE) Hebrews 13:1-2 (Let brotherly love continue. Do not neglect to show hospitality to strangers, for thereby some have entertained angels unawares.) We should continue to love one another as brothers and sisters love each other. We know this is one of the greatest commandments. We should also never fail to show kindness and love to those we do not know. As some have entertained angels without knowing it, we can show care and concern for any child of God. It benefits everyone and glorifies our Father in heaven.

- Broad application: Don't miss opportunities to care.
- Your application:

_____

_____

_____

_____

_____

_____

_____

_____

_____

_____

_____

_____

_____

_____

_____

_____

_____

JUNE 13:

(GO) Lamentations 3:25-26 (The Lord is good to those who wait for him, to the soul who seeks him. It is good that one should wait quietly for the salvation of the Lord.) The Lord is good to those who seek Him. He is good to those who wait for Him. He has only good things in store for us. It is good when we wait quietly for the salvation of the Lord. His grace sustains us.

- Broad application: It is good to wait.
- Your application:

_____

_____

_____

_____

_____

_____

_____

_____

_____

_____

_____

_____

_____

_____

_____

_____

_____

_____

JUNE 14:

(LS) 2 Corinthians 1:3-4 (Blessed be the God and Father of our Lord Jesus Christ, the Father of mercies and God of all comfort, who comforts us in all our affliction, so that we may be able to comfort those who are in any distress, with the ease with which we are comforted by God.) We praise God, the Father of our Lord and Savior, Jesus Christ. He is the Father of deliverance and the God who supplies us with total comfort. And as He eases our pain and suffering, we learn how to help others in theirs. Following the Lord will have its hardships. But He makes way for all of us to get what we need.

- Broad application: Turn to God for comfort.
- Your application:

_____

_____

_____

_____

_____

_____

_____

_____

_____

_____

_____

_____

_____

_____

_____

JUNE 15:

(L) Luke 6:35 (But love your enemies, and do good, and lend, expecting nothing in return, and your reward will be great, and you will be sons of the Most High, for he is kind to the ungrateful and the evil.) Love your enemies, do good, and lend, expecting nothing in return. These acts get rewarded because they show God's kind of love, agape love. God is kind to the ungrateful and evil. We should do the same.

- Broad application: Love the unkind.
- Your application:

_____

_____

_____

_____

_____

_____

_____

_____

_____

_____

_____

_____

_____

_____

_____

_____

_____

_____

_____

JUNE 16:

(M) Galatians 6:3-4 (If anyone thinks he is something when he is nothing, he deceives himself. But let each one test his work, and then his reason to boast will be in himself alone and not in his neighbor.) If we begin to think we are something, we are fooling ourselves. We are nothing without grace. But if we dare to examine ourselves, let us not compare ourselves to others. We should be humble enough to know our value is through Christ Jesus. We should boast because of that.

- Broad application: Examine yourself.
- Your application:

_____

_____

_____

_____

_____

_____

_____

_____

_____

_____

_____

_____

_____

_____

_____

_____

JUNE 17:

(P) Isaiah 57:20-21 (But the wicked are like the tossing sea; for it cannot be quiet, and its waters toss up mire and dirt. "There is no peace," says my God, "for the wicked.") When the sea is tossing, turning, and roaring it is picking up dirt and mess. It is not calm. It can't be quiet. God compares it to the wicked. They are never at peace.

- Broad application: Be still and experience peace.
- Your application:

_____

_____

_____

_____

_____

_____

_____

_____

_____

_____

_____

_____

_____

_____

_____

_____

_____

_____

_____

_____

JUNE 18:

(J) Proverbs 23:24 (The father of the righteous will greatly rejoice; he who fathers a wise son will be glad in him.) What a blessing it is to have a child who follows the Lord! It is a Christian parent's greatest desire. We also know the child will have access to God's abundant wisdom. What joy that brings to anyone's soul!

- Broad application: Rejoice for Godly children.
- Your application:

_____
_____
_____
_____
_____
_____
_____
_____
_____
_____
_____
_____
_____
_____
_____
_____
_____
_____
_____

June 19:

(T) 1 Thessalonians 5:21-22 (But test everything; hold fast what is good. Abstain from every form of evil.) Be mindful of what is good and holy. Sometimes the lines may be slightly blurred, so test whether it is of God through prayer and reference to His Word and His will. Hold on to what is good. Steer clear of every form of evil.

- Broad application: Test the waters.
- Your application:

_____

_____

_____

_____

_____

_____

_____

_____

_____

_____

_____

_____

_____

_____

_____

_____

_____

_____

_____

June 20:

(F) Galatians 3:22-23 (But Scripture has locked up everything under the control of sin, so that what it promised, being given through faith in Jesus Christ, might be given to those who believe. Before this faith, the law had us imprisoned. We could not escape until this faith in Jesus Christ set us free.) The law did not leave any room for transgressions, intentional or otherwise. No one could live up to what was asked of them to do. We were doomed. Therefore, faith in Jesus promised deliverance. Now, one only must believe to receive salvation.

- Broad application: Be thankful for faith.
- Your application:

_____

_____

_____

_____

_____

_____

_____

_____

_____

_____

_____

_____

_____

_____

_____

_____

JUNE 21:

(F) Hebrews 13:5-6 (Keep your life free from love of money, and be content with what you have, for he has said, "I will never leave you nor forsake you." So we can confidently say, "The Lord is my helper; I will not fear; what can man do to me?") When we have an excessive desire for things, it is not pleasing to God. We can be content with what we have. God's Word says He will provide us with everything we need. We can trust Him. We have nothing to fear.

- Broad application: Know how blessed you are.
- Your application:

_____
_____
_____
_____
_____
_____
_____
_____
_____
_____
_____
_____
_____
_____
_____
_____
_____
_____

JUNE 22:

(GE) Psalm 18:35-36 (You have given me the shield of your salvation, your right hand supported me, and your gentleness made me great. You showed a vast place for my steps under me, and my feet did not slip.) We have the Lord's protection through the gift of salvation. His right hand keeps us safe. His kindness makes us great. We can walk and be confident in His greatness. We can stand tall on His foundation.

- Broad application: Stand on the Rock.
- Your application:

_____

_____

_____

_____

_____

_____

_____

_____

_____

_____

_____

_____

_____

_____

_____

_____

_____

_____

_____

JUNE 23:

(GO) Micah 6:7-8 (Will the Lord be pleased with thousands of rams and ten thousand rivers of oil? Shall I give my firstborn for my transgression, the fruit of my body for the sin of my soul? He has told you, O man, what is good; and what does the Lord require of you but to do justice, love kindness, and walk humbly with your God?) We can not offer up to God anything of material value. We can not perform any ritual that would be sufficient in His eyes. The only good and perfect gifts we can give Him come from knowing Him. They come from being obedient to Him. We should do what is right, be kind, and humble ourselves before Him.

- Broad application: Present goodness.
- Your application:

_____
_____
_____
_____
_____
_____
_____
_____
_____
_____
_____
_____
_____
_____

JUNE 24:

(J) Psalm 28:6-7 (Blessed be the Lord! For he has heard the voice of my pleas for mercy. The Lord is my strength and shield; in him my heart trusts, and I receive help; my heart exults, and with my song, I give thanks to him.) Praise the Lord! He hears our pleas for mercy. In Him, we find strength and protection. We trust that He will help us. Our hearts fill with joy, and we sing praises to Him.

- Broad application: Sing praises to the Lord.
- Your application:

_____
_____
_____
_____
_____
_____
_____
_____
_____
_____
_____
_____
_____
_____
_____
_____
_____
_____
_____
_____

JUNE 25:

(LS) Psalm 34:18-19 (The Lord stays close to the brokenhearted and rescues the spirit of the crushed. The righteous may have many afflictions, but the Lord delivers him out of them all.) The Lord is never far from us when our hearts are troubled by sadness, disappointments, and guilt. We can find Him close by when we are in physical danger or need spiritual guidance. Every second of every day, we need His help. Being made righteous through Him has its challenges. But the Lord is there to pull us through every time.

- Broad application: Count on His presence.
- Your application:

_____

_____

_____

_____

_____

_____

_____

_____

_____

_____

_____

_____

_____

_____

_____

_____

_____

June 26:

(L) I Corinthians 13:4-5 (Love is patient and kind; love does not envy or boast; it is not arrogant or rude. It does not insist on its way; it is not irritable or resentful.) God's love, agape love, is expressed as being kind and tolerant. So it is not jealous or prideful. There is no reason for it to be arrogant or impolite. It considers the rights and needs of others. And it is not easily provoked or bitter.

- Broad application: Know the ways of love.
- Your application:

_____
_____
_____
_____
_____
_____
_____
_____
_____
_____
_____
_____
_____
_____
_____
_____
_____
_____
_____

JUNE 27:

(M) Philippians 2:2-3 (Complete my joy by agreeing, having the same love, being in full accord and of one mind. Do nothing from selfish ambition or conceit, but in humility count others more significant than yourselves.) Paul tells the Philippians that his happiness would be complete if they were on one accord and had the same love. He says they could accomplish this love by not being selfish and arrogant. If they humbled themselves before God, they would consider others. The needs and problems of others would be their priority. Their Christian brothers and sisters would be more important than themselves.

- Broad application: Don't dwell on self.
- Your application:

_____
_____
_____
_____
_____
_____
_____
_____
_____
_____
_____
_____
_____
_____
_____
_____
_____

JUNE 28:

(P) Ephesians 2:14-15 (He is our peace. He made us one by breaking down the dividing wall of hostility. Jesus came in the flesh to release us from the weight of the law. He provided a way for us to finally be at peace with each other.) The Lord Jesus Christ is the source of our tranquility. Through Him, Jews and Gentiles are brought together as one body. The law is no longer a source of division and hostility. Through the death of our Savior, the law has reached fulfillment. The new body is the Christian church.

- Broad application: Live in perfect peace.
- Your application:

_____

_____

_____

_____

_____

_____

_____

_____

_____

_____

_____

_____

_____

_____

_____

JUNE 29:

(T) James 1:19-20 (Know this, my beloved brothers: let every person be quick to hear, slow to speak, slow to anger; for man's anger does not produce the righteousness of God.) As we go through trials, we need to seek God's wisdom. We need to be able to hear God's plan. Wisdom tells us to remain quiet and listen to God's instructions. We should be slow to speak because it may lead to anger. Anger, in turn, may drown out the will of God.

- Broad application: Stop and listen for God.
- Your application:

_____
_____
_____
_____
_____
_____
_____
_____
_____
_____
_____
_____
_____
_____
_____
_____
_____
_____

JUNE 30:

(F) Psalm 145:18-19 (The Lord is near to all who call on him, to all who call on him in truth. He fulfills the desire of those who fear him; he also hears their cry and saves them.) We trust these things. The Lord is never far away from those of us who call on Him. He is there when we sincerely seek Him. God gives us what we desire when we walk according to His will. He also hears our concerns and delivers us.

- Broad application: Stand on His Word.
- Your application:

_____

_____

_____

_____

_____

_____

_____

_____

_____

_____

_____

_____

_____

_____

_____

_____

_____

_____

July 1:

(F) Matthew 6:25-26 ("Therefore I tell you, do not be anxious about your life, what you will eat or what you will drink, nor about your body, what you will put on. Is not life more than food and the body more than clothing? Look at the birds of the air: they neither sow nor reap nor gather into barns, yet your heavenly Father feeds them. Are you not of more value than they?") It is dangerous to allow ourselves to worry about our day-to-day needs. There is more to life than that! Worry will cause us to miss out on God's spiritual blessings. If we look around at the birds in the air, God takes care of everything He created, regardless. Unarguably, our souls are of much greater value to Him than they are.

- Broad application: Reference nature.
- Your application:

_____
_____
_____
_____
_____
_____
_____
_____
_____
_____
_____
_____
_____

JULY 2:

(GE) John 19:27 (Then he said to the disciple, "Behold, your mother!" And from that hour, the disciple took her to his own home.) Amidst His pain and suffering, Jesus was concerned about His mother's well-being. He made sure she would be taken in by His trusted disciple John. John would treat her as his mother. No questions asked.

- Broad application: Treat others like family.
- Your application:

_____

_____

_____

_____

_____

_____

_____

_____

_____

_____

_____

_____

_____

_____

_____

_____

_____

_____

_____

July 3:

(GO) 1 Corinthians 15:33-34 (Do not be deceived. Bad company ruins good morals. Wake up from your drunken stupor, as is right, and do not go on sinning. Some do not know God. I say this to your shame.) Don't kid yourself. Being in the company of those who do evil can corrupt one's morals. So wake up and practice righteous behavior. Some people do not know God. It may be hard to believe as Christians, but it's true.

- Broad application: Run with the righteous.
- Your application:

_____
_____
_____
_____
_____
_____
_____
_____
_____
_____
_____
_____
_____
_____
_____
_____
_____
_____
_____
_____
_____

JULY 4:

(L) John 3:16 ("For God so loved the world, that he gave his only Son, that whoever believes in him should not perish but have eternal life.") God sending Jesus is the ultimate show of God's love for us. We are brought back into His good graces through Jesus's willingness to do His Father's will. Christ bridged the gap. Eternal life with our Creator is where we yearn to be.

- Broad application: Show life-changing love.
- Your application:

_____

_____

_____

_____

_____

_____

_____

_____

_____

_____

_____

_____

_____

_____

_____

_____

_____

_____

_____

July 5:

(J) Ecclesiastes 7:13-14 (Consider the work of God: who can make straight what he has crooked? In the day of prosperity, be joyful, and in the day of adversity, consider: God has made the one and the other, so that man may not find out anything that will be after him.) When we believe in God's work, we must know He has a hand in everything. His divine will rules. We can not fix what He has set in motion. God makes each day, whether we consider it a good one or a bad one. But our joy should be in knowing He is still omnipotent.

- Broad application: Know who has the power.
- Your application:

_____
_____
_____
_____
_____
_____
_____
_____
_____
_____
_____
_____
_____
_____
_____
_____

JULY 6:

(LS) Isaiah 48:10-11 (Behold, I have refined you, but not as silver; I have tried you in the furnace of affliction. I do it for my own sake, for how should my name be profaned? My glory I will not give to another.) God is constantly polishing us up. He is weeding out our impurities daily. Our trials and ordeals are getting us ready for His glory. No one will be able to steal His thunder! Everyone will know His work, and He is God!

- Broad application: Let the Lord use you.
- Your application:

_____
_____
_____
_____
_____
_____
_____
_____
_____
_____
_____
_____
_____
_____
_____
_____
_____
_____

JULY 7:

(M) 2 Chronicles 7:14-15 (If my people who are called by my name humble themselves, pray, seek my face, and turn from their wicked ways, then I will hear from heaven, forgive their sin, and heal their land. Now my eyes will be open, and my ears will be attentive to the prayer in this place.) Initially, God gave this promise to the people of Israel, but it is still valid for God's people today. As Christians, we are called by His name. So God is always ready to hear a word from us. He patiently waits for us to swallow our pride, pray, seek His will, and repent. Only then will our sins be forgiven and healing begin.

- Broad application: Submit, pray, seek, repent, heal.
- Your application:

_____

_____

_____

_____

_____

_____

_____

_____

_____

_____

_____

_____

_____

_____

_____

_____

JULY 8:

(P) Isaiah 32:17-18 (The fruit of that righteousness will be peace; its effect will be quietness and confidence forever. My people will abide in peaceful habitations, secure dwellings, and quiet resting places.) When we work toward righteousness, we will be at peace. And because of that peace, we will find ourselves in a calm and secure place. A quiet place. A place where we can be at rest. We can have that peaceful home here on earth.

- Broad application: Find your quiet place.
- Your application:

_____

_____

_____

_____

_____

_____

_____

_____

_____

_____

_____

_____

_____

_____

_____

_____

_____

_____

July 9:

(T) James 1:21-22) (Therefore put away all filthiness and rampant wickedness and receive with meekness the implanted Word, which can save your souls. But be doers of the Word, and not hearers only, deceiving yourselves.) Steer clear of anything indecent. Avoid widespread evil. Welcome the Word of God with all humility because it is the way to salvation. Apply what we have heard and learned. Do not fool ourselves into believing it can work any other way.

- Broad application: Be rooted in the Word.
- Your application:

_____

_____

_____

_____

_____

_____

_____

_____

_____

_____

_____

_____

_____

_____

_____

_____

_____

_____

_____

JULY 10:

(F) Romans 8:38-39 (For I am sure that neither death nor life, nor angels nor rulers, nor things present nor things to come, nor powers, nor height nor depth, nor anything else in all creation, will be able to separate us from the love of God in Christ Jesus our Lord.) Absolutely nothing can separate us from the love of God. Life cannot; death cannot. Nothing on earth or in heaven, whether now or in the future, can interfere with His love for us. It is solid. Jesus Christ made that possible.

- Broad application: Because He said so!
- Your application:

_____
_____
_____
_____
_____
_____
_____
_____
_____
_____
_____
_____
_____
_____
_____
_____
_____

JULY 11:

(F) Matthew 10:34-45 ("Do not think I have come to bring peace on earth. I have not come to bring peace but a sword. I have set a man against his father, a daughter against her mother, and a daughter against her mother-in-law.") Jesus is the ultimate Prince of Peace. However, Jesus came to fulfill the law, and in doing so, there was division even among family members. Some rejected Him; some didn't. But neither family loyalty nor social traditions should sway our allegiance to God. He deserves our complete devotion.

- Broad application: Be all in.
- Your application:

_____

_____

_____

_____

_____

_____

_____

_____

_____

_____

_____

_____

_____

_____

_____

_____

_____

July 12:

(GE) Acts 28:2 (The native people showed us unusual kindness, for they kindled a fire and welcomed us all because it had begun to rain and was cold.) Paul and his party get shipwrecked on the island of Melita. The natives, of course, did not know them, but they were exceptionally kind to them. They welcomed them and built a fire to keep them warm from the cold and rain. The people showed Paul and his companions God-like kindness during their stay.

- Broad application: Kindness knows no stranger.
- Your application:

_____
_____
_____
_____
_____
_____
_____
_____
_____
_____
_____
_____
_____
_____
_____
_____
_____
_____

JULY 13:

(GO) Ephesians 4:30-31 (And do not grieve the Holy Spirit of God, because the seal is there for the day of redemption. Get rid of all bitterness, wrath, anger, clamor, and slander from you, along with all malice.) The Holy Spirit was left to comfort and guide us until the end. We should not deny it. By allowing the Spirit to work in our lives, we become perfected, more Christ-like. It is part of our Christian journey. Bitterness, anger, turmoil, lies, and hatred should become things of the past.

- Broad application: Take advantage of the Spirit.
- Your application:

_____
_____
_____
_____
_____
_____
_____
_____
_____
_____
_____
_____
_____
_____
_____
_____
_____

JULY 14:

(J) Luke 15:6-7 ("And when he comes home, he calls his friends and his neighbors, saying to them, 'Rejoice with me, for I have found my sheep that was lost.' Just so, I tell you, there will be more joy in heaven over one sinner who repents than over ninety-nine righteous persons who need no repentance.") How many of us have lost something valuable? And how many of us remember how it felt when we found it? Jesus is concerned about our souls. He, our Father, the Holy Spirit, and all the saints leap with joy when just one of us repents and no longer follows the devil. Know that heaven will be having a hallelujah good time!

- Broad application: Keep ministering to the lost.
- Your application:

_____
_____
_____
_____
_____
_____
_____
_____
_____
_____
_____
_____
_____
_____
_____
_____

July 15:

(LS) Romans 8:17-18 (And if children, then heirs-heirs of God and fellow heirs with Christ, provided we suffer with him so that we may also have the glory with him. I consider that the sufferings of this present time are not worth comparing with the glory to be revealed to us.) As children of God, we receive blessings as heirs of God. We, in turn, are blessed to be joint heirs of Jesus Christ. Our sufferings with Jesus make that so. Our sacrifices can never be in vain. We will have our reward in God's kingdom, where His wondrous glory gets revealed.

- Broad application: Anticipate God's glory.
- Your application:

_____
_____
_____
_____
_____
_____
_____
_____
_____
_____
_____
_____
_____
_____
_____
_____
_____
_____

JULY 16:

(L) Matthew 5:38-39 ("You have heard that it was said, 'An eye for an eye and a tooth for a tooth.' But I say to you, Do not resist the evil one. But if anyone slaps you on the right cheek, turn to him the other also.") Jesus reminds us not to retaliate, no matter what we may have heard. Our natural (sinful) impulse is to strike back. But He instructs us to love, not hate. He does not want us to seek vengeance. We should follow Jesus's example.

- Broad application: Do as Jesus would.
- Your application:

_____
_____
_____
_____
_____
_____
_____
_____
_____
_____
_____
_____
_____
_____
_____
_____

July 17:

(M) 1 Peter 2:1-2 (So put away all malice, deceit, hypocrisy, envy, and slander. Like newborn infants, long for the pure spiritual milk, that by it you may grow up into salvation.) If we humble ourselves before the Lord, some things can't coexist. Hatred, deception, hypocrisy, jealousy, and slander have to go! We need to come before the Lord as infants, seeking the spiritual nourishment of our Creator. We need His food to make us big and strong in the Word. We need nutrition that will lead us to eternal life.

- Broad application: Crave God's Word.
- Your application:

_____
_____
_____
_____
_____
_____
_____
_____
_____
_____
_____
_____
_____
_____
_____
_____

JULY 18:

(P) Matthew 5:9-10 ("Blessed are the peacemakers, for they shall be called sons of God. Blessed are those who are persecuted for righteousness sake, for theirs is the kingdom of heaven.") When we give our lives to God, we desire the same kind of peace that knowing Him gives us. We become "peacemakers" in a world that has none. As children of God, it is a blessing to take on this responsibility. And in doing so, we will be persecuted for doing the right thing in an unrighteous world. But it's even more definite that we will be rewarded as heirs to God's kingdom for all eternity.

- Broad application: Boldly be a peacemaker.
- Your application:

_____
_____
_____
_____
_____
_____
_____
_____
_____
_____
_____
_____
_____
_____
_____

July 19:

(J) Psalm 117 (Praise the Lord, all nations! Extol him, all peoples! For great is his steadfast love toward us, and the faithfulness of the Lord endures forever. Praise the Lord!) The Lord is the only one who deserves this much praise! So praise the Lord, all nations! Glorify Him, everybody! His unwavering love for us is excellent, and His commitment to us is forever. Praise His holy name!

- Broad application: Uplift Him!
- Your application:

_____
_____
_____
_____
_____
_____
_____
_____
_____
_____
_____
_____
_____
_____
_____
_____
_____
_____
_____
_____

JULY 20:

(F) Romans 8:26-27 (Likewise, the Spirit helps us in our weakness. For we do not know what to pray for as we ought, but the Spirit himself intercedes for us with groanings too deep for words. And he who searches hearts knows what is the mind of the Spirit, because the Spirit intercedes for the saints according to the will of God.) The Holy Spirit is our comforter and strength. A great example is when we want to pray but are at a loss for words. The Spirit steps in and makes our petitions known to our Father. The Spirit knows everything. We can rest assured that God hears our needs and desires.

- Broad application: Trust, no words are needed.
- Your application:

_____
_____
_____
_____
_____
_____
_____
_____
_____
_____
_____
_____
_____
_____
_____

JULY 21:

(F) Psalm 27:4-5 (One thing have I asked of the Lord, that will I seek after: that I may dwell in the house of the Lord all the days of my life, to gaze upon the beauty of the Lord and to inquire in his temple. He will hide me in his shelter in the day of trouble, conceal me under his tent; he will lift me high upon a rock.) When we seek and ask for refuge, we can be sure to find comfort and security in God's spiritual house every day. While there, we can enjoy the beauty of being in His presence. There we can ask Him anything we want. He will cover us with His protective arms. He will support us so we will not fall.

- Broad application: Trust God as your host.
- Your application:

_____

_____

_____

_____

_____

_____

_____

_____

_____

_____

_____

_____

_____

_____

_____

_____

JULY 22:

(L) Isaiah 49:15-16 (Can a woman forget her nursing child, that she should have no compassion on the son of her womb? Even these may forget, yet I will not forget you. Behold, I have engraved you on the palms of my hands; your walls are continually before me.) It is hard for us to imagine a mother forgetting her child. It is tough to comprehend this when the child is still needing to be nursed by the mother. Surely she would love him enough to give him food. But even if she did, there is no chance our heavenly Father would ever forget us. We are embedded in His loving hands and forever under His protection.

- Broad application: Be as inseparable from God.
- Your application:

_____
_____
_____
_____
_____
_____
_____
_____
_____
_____
_____
_____
_____
_____
_____

July 23:

(GO) Luke 6:43-44 ("For no good tree bears bad fruit, nor again does a bad tree bear good fruit, for each tree is known by its fruit. For figs are not gathered from thornbushes, nor are grapes picked from a bramble bush.") These are the fruit of the Spirit: love, joy, peace, long-suffering, gentleness, goodness, faith, meekness, and temperance. The world will know who we genuinely serve by the fruit we produce. It is just that simple. The fruit of the Spirit is from God. Evil and corruption are the fruit of the devil.

- Broad application: Bear good fruit.
- Your application:

_____

_____

_____

_____

_____

_____

_____

_____

_____

_____

_____

_____

_____

_____

_____

_____

_____

_____

JULY 24:

(J) Ecclesiastes 3:12-13 (I perceived that there is nothing better for them than to be joyful and to do good as long as they live, also that everyone should eat and drink and take pleasure in all his toil-this is God's gift to man.) God wants us to have joy in our lives. He wants us to do good things. God also wants us to eat, drink, and be happy in our work. These are all gifts he gives to us freely. He doesn't want to hold anything back from us that is pleasing in His sight.

- Broad application: Experience God's gifts.
- Your application:

_____
_____
_____
_____
_____
_____
_____
_____
_____
_____
_____
_____
_____
_____
_____
_____
_____
_____

July 25:

(LS) 1 Peter 5:10-11 (And after you have suffered a little while, the God of all grace, who has called you to his eternal glory in Christ, will himself restore, confirm, strengthen, and establish you. To him be the dominion forever and ever. Amen.) We will suffer for a while here on earth. But God's grace will be enough to carry us through. Our patience will give us increased faith. God will renew our strength. To God be the power and glory!

- Broad application: Hold on and endure.
- Your application:

_____
_____
_____
_____
_____
_____
_____
_____
_____
_____
_____
_____
_____
_____
_____
_____
_____
_____

JULY 26:

(L) 1 John 2:9-10 (Whoever says he is in the light and hates his brother is still in darkness. Whoever loves his brother abides in the glow of the morning, and in him, there is no cause for stumbling.) There is no way we can be in the presence of God and not love our fellow man. If we say we do not love our brother, we are far from God. We are in darkness. If we love our brother, we are in the presence of God, where there is light to keep us from tripping up.

- Broad application: Walk in His light.
- Your application:

_____
_____
_____
_____
_____
_____
_____
_____
_____
_____
_____
_____
_____
_____
_____
_____
_____
_____

JULY 27:

(M) Jeremiah 9:23-24 (Thus says the Lord, "Let not the wise man boast in his wisdom, let not the mighty man boast in his might, let not the rich man boast in his riches, but let him who boasts boast in this, that he understands and knows me, that I am the Lord who practices steadfast love, justice, and righteousness in the earth. For in these things I delight," declares the Lord.) If a man is wise, firm, or prosperous, there is still no need for him to boast about these things. He should be thankful that he knows the one and only true God. He should praise God for His steadfast love for him. He should praise Him for being a just and righteous God. These qualities are gifts from Him to us.

- Broad application: Boast about God.
- Your application:

_____
_____
_____
_____
_____
_____
_____
_____
_____
_____
_____
_____
_____
_____

JULY 28:

(P) Isaiah 53:4-5 (Surely he has borne our griefs and carried our sorrows; yet we esteemed him stricken, smitten by God, and afflicted. But he was pierced for our transgressions; was crushed for our iniquities; upon him was the chastisement that brought us peace, and with his wounds, we found healing.) Jesus took on all the griefs and sorrows associated with sin. But not for any of His sins, for our sins! He suffered dearly on our behalf. We now have eternal peace with God through His horrifying punishment and death. Jesus' physical wounds healed our spiritual wounds.

- Broad application: Remember the price of peace.
- Your application:

_____

_____

_____

_____

_____

_____

_____

_____

_____

_____

_____

_____

_____

_____

_____

_____

JULY 29:

(T) Proverbs 18:20-21 (From the fruit of a man's mouth, his stomach is satisfied; his help is from the yield of his lips. Death and life are in the power of the tongue, and those who love it will eat its fruit.) When we speak sensibly and thoughtfully, it is satisfying to our souls. When our speech is righteous, it can be uplifting and valuable to ourselves and others. Our tongue has the power to destroy or save. God will hold us accountable for our words as well as our actions. We can use them for good or evil.

- Broad application: Pray to control your tongue.
- Your application:

_____
_____
_____
_____
_____
_____
_____
_____
_____
_____
_____
_____
_____
_____
_____
_____

JULY 30:

(F) Matthew 19:26 (But Jesus looked at them and said, "With man this is impossible, but with God all things are possible.") Here, Jesus is responding to His disciples' question regarding the rich and salvation. Jesus corrected the people's notion that God blesses the rich, and therefore they are automatically saved. But even though it is harder for the rich to enter heaven's kingdom, it is not impossible. With God, everything is possible.

- Broad application: Know He can.
- Your application:

_____
_____
_____
_____
_____
_____
_____
_____
_____
_____
_____
_____
_____
_____
_____
_____
_____
_____

JULY 31:

(F) John 3:18 ("Whoever believes in him is not condemned, but whoever does not believe is condemned already because he has not
believed in the name of the only Son of God.") Jesus Christ died for
the pardon of our sins. If we believe in Him, we are no longer doomed.
But if we do not believe in Him, we are already lost. Eternal life is for
those who believe.

- Broad application: Believe in His name.
- Your application:

_____

_____

_____

_____

_____

_____

_____

_____

_____

_____

_____

_____

_____

_____

_____

_____

_____

_____

_____

AUGUST 1:

(GE) Job 10:12 (You have granted me life and steadfast love, and your care has preserved my spirit.) God gave us life. He showers us with His never-ending love. The deep concern He has for us feeds our souls and maintains our spirits. We can emulate God's devotion and kindness.

- Broad application: Pass it on.
- Your application:

_____

_____

_____

_____

_____

_____

_____

_____

_____

_____

_____

_____

_____

_____

_____

_____

_____

_____

_____

_____

AUGUST 2:

(GO) Genesis 50:20 (You intended to harm me, but God intended it for good to save many lives.) Because of their jealousy toward Joseph, his brothers tried to get rid of him. But later, Joseph, governor of Egypt, was able to help his brothers and their families during the famine. He did not rub it in their faces or take any credit for it. He just told them how the goodness of God prevails no matter what.

- Broad application: Don't waste time on evil.
- Your application:

_____
_____
_____
_____
_____
_____
_____
_____
_____
_____
_____
_____
_____
_____
_____
_____
_____
_____

August 3:

(J) Psalm 149:4-5 (For the Lord takes pleasure in his people; he adorns the humble with salvation. Let the godly exult in glory, let them sing for joy on their beds.) The Lord is glad we are His people. And we are so happy He has given us the gift of salvation. We are in awe of His mercy. We have tremendous joy in His presence. We praise Him well into the night.

- Broad application: Have late-night praise.
- Your application:

_____

_____

_____

_____

_____

_____

_____

_____

_____

_____

_____

_____

_____

_____

_____

_____

_____

_____

AUGUST 4:

(LS) Isaiah 40:30-31 (Even youths shall faint and be weary, and young men shall fall exhausted. But they who wait for the Lord shall renew their strength and mount with wings like eagles. They shall run and not be weary; they shall walk and not faint.) Even the young get weak and tired. But we who patiently put our faith and trust in the Lord will find renewed strength. The Lord will give us His brand of power to persevere on our journey, each of us according to our spiritual pace. Some will be able to run; some will walk, but none will faint.

- Broad application: Receive God's second wind.
- Your application:

_____

_____

_____

_____

_____

_____

_____

_____

_____

_____

_____

_____

_____

_____

_____

_____

_____

_____

August 5:

(L) Romans 13:9-10 (For the commandments, "You shall not commit adultery, You shall not murder, You shall not steal, You shall not covet," and any other commandment, are summed up in this word: "You shall love your neighbor as yourself." Love does no wrong to a neighbor; therefore, love is the fulfilling of the law.") We shall not commit adultery, murder, steal, or desire what our neighbor has. All the commandments hinge on one, love our neighbor as ourselves. If we love our neighbor as we love ourselves, we will not harm him. Love completes the law. Love is all God requires.

- Broad application: Remember this one commandment.
- Your application:

_____

_____

_____

_____

_____

_____

_____

_____

_____

_____

_____

_____

_____

_____

AUGUST 6:

(M) Luke 22:26 ("But not so with you. Rather, let the greatest among you become the youngest, and the leader as one who serves.") We are not here to obtain titles, power, or praise. We are here to serve as Jesus served. As Christians, this is our responsibility as we show others the ways of the Lord. No one is greater than the other when we all humble ourselves for service.

- Broad application: Just serve.
- Your application:

_____
_____
_____
_____
_____
_____
_____
_____
_____
_____
_____
_____
_____
_____
_____
_____
_____
_____

AUGUST 7:

(P) Proverbs 3:1-2 (My son, do not forget my teaching, but let your heart keep my commandments, for long days and years of life and peace they will add to you.) God has given us His Word for our benefit and protection. So we should do our best to remember His commandments. We should keep them in our hearts to easily apply them. God promises that we will have added days we do this. He will fill our lives with peace.

- Broad application: Know it's a heart thing.
- Your application:

_____

_____

_____

_____

_____

_____

_____

_____

_____

_____

_____

_____

_____

_____

_____

_____

_____

AUGUST 8:

(T) Ecclesiastes 11:9-10 (Rejoice, O young man, in your youth, and let your heart cheer you in the days as a child. Walk in the ways of your heart and the sight of your eyes. But know that God will bring you into judgment for all these things. Remove vexation from your heart, and put away pain from your body, for youth and the dawn of life are vanity.) Being young can be a fun and happy time in our lives. So when we are physically young (or even young in the faith), it is easy to get caught up in what the heart wants and the eyes see. But know that God will still hold us accountable for our actions. So we should not be anxious when we are "missing out" on something or practicing self-control. In the end, it is all vanity anyway.

- Broad application: Don't waste your youth.
- Your application:

_____

_____

_____

_____

_____

_____

_____

_____

_____

_____

_____

_____

_____

_____

AUGUST 9:

(L) Philippians 2:4-5 (Let each of you look not only to his interests but also to the interests of others. Have this mind among yourselves, which is yours in Christ Jesus.) Paul again is talking to the church here. The Christian mindset should care for others, not just us. We should seek out those in need, especially in the faith community. The need to show love and support is crucial among believers. It is an example that was set forth by Christ himself.

- Broad application: Think of others.
- Your application:

_____

_____

_____

_____

_____

_____

_____

_____

_____

_____

_____

_____

_____

_____

_____

_____

_____

_____

AUGUST 10:

(F) 1 Corinthians 16:13 (Be watchful, stand firm in the faith, act like men, be strong.) We should always examine our thoughts and actions. We need to be unwavering in the decisions we make. We should act like adults and seek God's wisdom. We should be courageous and strong.

- Broad application: Watch. Stand. Grow. Strengthen.
- Your application:

_____

_____

_____

_____

_____

_____

_____

_____

_____

_____

_____

_____

_____

_____

_____

_____

_____

_____

_____

_____

_____

_____

AUGUST 11:

(GE) Colossians 3:13 (...bearing with one another and, if one has a complaint against another, forgiving each other; as the Lord has forgiven you, so you also must forgive.) We are all flawed. Yet the Lord is still merciful and forgiving. So we should be the same toward our brothers and sisters. It should be our prayer.

- Broad application: Always be merciful and forgiving.
- Your application:

_____

_____

_____

_____

_____

_____

_____

_____

_____

_____

_____

_____

_____

_____

_____

_____

_____

_____

_____

AUGUST 12:

(GO) Acts 20:35 (In all things I have shown you that by working hard in this way we must help the weak and remember the words of the Lord Jesus, how he said, "It is more blessed to give than to receive.") Giving God's gifts is much better than receiving them. It is a blessing to be a blessing to others. It is our Christian duty to help those who are less fortunate. We should be grateful because we have it to give.

- Broad application: Try to beat God's giving.
- Your application:

_____

_____

_____

_____

_____

_____

_____

_____

_____

_____

_____

_____

_____

_____

_____

_____

_____

_____

AUGUST 13:

(J) Revelation 21:3-4 (I heard a loud voice from the throne saying, "Behold, the dwelling place of God is with man. He will dwell with them, and they will be his people, and God himself will be with them as their God. He will wipe away every tear from their eyes, and death shall be no more, neither shall there be mourning, nor crying, nor pain anymore, for the former things have passed away.") God will finally unite with His people. We will have eternal fellowship with Him. There will no longer be any reason for us to cry. There will be no more pain, sorrow, or death. There will be indescribable joy.

- Broad application: Imagine that day!
- Your application:

_____

_____

_____

_____

_____

_____

_____

_____

_____

_____

_____

_____

_____

_____

_____

_____

AUGUST 14:

(LS) 1 Peter 2:19-20 (For this is a gracious thing, when, mindful of God, one endures sorrows while suffering unjustly. What credit is it if you hold on when you sin and suffer for it? But if you do good and suffer for it, you endure. This suffering is a gracious thing in the sight of God.) It is not a noble thing when we bear the punishment for our sins. The punishment fits the crime. But it _is_ a good thing when we suffer for the will of God. It is honorable to persevere for such a worthy cause. We should be incredibly thankful for the opportunity to live through the heartache and despair we will experience because of our commitment to Him.

- Broad application: Rise to the occasion.
- Your application:

_____

_____

_____

_____

_____

_____

_____

_____

_____

_____

_____

_____

_____

_____

_____

_____

AUGUST 15:

(L) 1 Samuel 12:23-24 (Moreover, as for me, far be it from me that I should sin against the Lord by ceasing to pray for you, and I will instruct you in the good and the right way. Only fear the Lord and serve him faithfully with all your heart. Consider what great things he has done for you.) We should care enough for our Christian brothers and sisters to keep them in our prayers. We should pray diligently for them, especially when they fall along the way. We should also continue to offer loving guidance to them when needed. We should teach them to fear the Lord and serve only Him. We should remind them how much He has done for us all.

- Broad application: Pray and teach.
- Your application:

_____
_____
_____
_____
_____
_____
_____
_____
_____
_____
_____
_____
_____
_____

AUGUST 16:

(M) Proverbs 16:19 (It is better to be of a lowly spirit with the poor than to divide the spoil with the proud.) We should be humble as the poor. The poor tend not to think too highly of themselves. In doing so, they can benefit from God's grace and mercy through their reliance on Him. On the other hand, sharing the spoils with the proud is not beneficial to us at all.

- Broad application: Learn from the poor.
- Your application:

_____

_____

_____

_____

_____

_____

_____

_____

_____

_____

_____

_____

_____

_____

_____

_____

_____

_____

AUGUST 17:

(P) Romans 12:18-19 (If possible, so far as it depends on you, live peaceably with all. Beloved, never avenge yourselves, but leave it to the wrath of God, for he has said, "Vengeance is mine, I will repay, says the Lord.") We should do everything we can to live in peace. That is our Christian duty. We aren't sure we can help with seeking retribution. That is up to the Lord. He is the only fair and just one.

- Broad application: Don't retaliate.
- Your application:

_____
_____
_____
_____
_____
_____
_____
_____
_____
_____
_____
_____
_____
_____
_____
_____
_____
_____

AUGUST 18:

(T) Proverbs 5:15-16 (Drink water from your cistern, flowing water from your well. Should your springs be scattered abroad, streams of water in the streets?) Having sexual desires is part of the human condition. God is aware of this because we are His design. And because He is a loving God, He has made provisions for this through marriage. Children should also come from the marriage union. Procreation is also God's design.

- Broad application: Follow God's perfect plan.
- Your application:

_____

_____

_____

_____

_____

_____

_____

_____

_____

_____

_____

_____

_____

_____

_____

_____

_____

AUGUST 19:

(L) Genesis 45:4-5 (Joseph said to his brothers, "Come near to me, please." And they came near. And he said, "I am your brother, Joseph, whom you sold into Egypt. And now do not be distressed or angry with yourselves because you sold me here, for God sent me before you to preserve life.") Joseph did not try to get back at his brothers for selling him into slavery. He also did not want them to be angry with themselves for their actions. Joseph knew everything that happened was for a reason. He knew God had a much bigger plan. His love and faith in God prevailed.

- Broad application: See the big picture.
- Your application:

_____

_____

_____

_____

_____

_____

_____

_____

_____

_____

_____

_____

_____

_____

AUGUST 20:

(F) 1 Timothy 4:12 (Let no one despise you for your youth, but set the believers an example in speech, conduct, love, faith, and purity.) Do not contribute to people discounting you because of your youth. Set an example for others through your words and actions. Be a good role model by loving others no matter what. Have faith in God in all situations.

- Broad application: Start young.
- Your application:

_____

_____

_____

_____

_____

_____

_____

_____

_____

_____

_____

_____

_____

_____

_____

_____

_____

_____

_____

_____

AUGUST 21:

(GE) Romans 14:1 (As for the one who is weak in faith, welcome him, but not to quarrel over opinions.) Our measure of faith in certain areas differs from the next person's level of dedication. Some of us are weak in specific things; others are strong. If we encounter someone vulnerable where we are strong, we should kindly welcome them. Our Christian goal is not to argue over their opinions or convictions.

- Broad application: Let them be.
- Your application:

_____
_____
_____
_____
_____
_____
_____
_____
_____
_____
_____
_____
_____
_____
_____
_____
_____
_____

AUGUST 22:

(GO) Proverbs 31:8 (Open your mouth for the mute, for the rights of all who are destitute.) We should stand up for those who cannot stand for themselves. We should speak up for those not heard. We should speak up for those who cannot speak for themselves. We should champion the rights of all God's children in need.

- Broad application: Show up for others.
- Your application:

_____
_____
_____
_____
_____
_____
_____
_____
_____
_____
_____
_____
_____
_____
_____
_____
_____
_____
_____

AUGUST 23:

(L) Ecclesiastes 11:1-2 (Cast your bread upon the waters, for you will find it after many days. Give a portion to seven, or even to eight, for you know not what disaster may happen on earth.) Bread can save lives. And it can come in any form (food, money, shelter, clothing, etc.). There are many people in need of assistance due to sin or natural disasters. But when we give, we can surely expect to be blessed in return, no matter how long it takes. God's Word assures us of this.

- Broad application: Be bread to someone.
- Your application:

_____
_____
_____
_____
_____
_____
_____
_____
_____
_____
_____
_____
_____
_____
_____
_____
_____

AUGUST 24:

(LS) James 5:7-8 (Be patient, therefore, brothers, until the coming of the Lord. See how the farmer waits for the precious fruit of the earth, being patient about it until it receives the early and the late rains. You also be patient. Establish your hearts, for the coming of the Lord is at hand.) Yes, patience is a virtue. It is a good and righteous thing. As the farmer calmly waits for the rains to yield good fruit, we should remain with the Lord. We should set our hearts on this. His return is near.

- Broad application: Wait for your reward.
- Your application:

_____

_____

_____

_____

_____

_____

_____

_____

_____

_____

_____

_____

_____

_____

_____

_____

_____

_____

August 25:

(L) Proverbs 3:3-4 (Let not steadfast love and faithfulness forsake you; bind them around your neck; write them on the tablet of your heart. So you will find favor and success in the sight of God and man.) Never set aside love and being faithful to the Word. Keep them close to us. Please keep them in our hearts. Love and truth will serve us well as followers of Christ. They will serve us well as leaders of men.

- Broad application: Cling to love and truth.
- Your application:

_____

_____

_____

_____

_____

_____

_____

_____

_____

_____

_____

_____

_____

_____

_____

_____

_____

_____

AUGUST 26:

(M) Romans 8:7 (For the mind that stays on the flesh is hostile to God, for it does not submit to God's law; indeed, it cannot.) When our minds focus on carnal thoughts, we are not in line with the will of God. We are at odds with it. We cannot submit to Him under these conditions. Only allowing the Holy Spirit to intervene can change the course of that.

- Broad application: Submit for a change.
- Your application:

_____

_____

_____

_____

_____

_____

_____

_____

_____

_____

_____

_____

_____

_____

_____

_____

_____

_____

AUGUST 27:

(L) Exodus 13:17-18 (When Pharaoh let the people go, God did not lead them by way of the land of the Philistines, although that was near. For God said, "Lest the people change their minds when they see war and return to Egypt." But God led the people around by way of the wilderness toward the Red Sea. And the people of Israel went up out of the land of Egypt equipped for battle.) When Pharaoh let the people go, God's love for them was still ordering their every step. He loved them enough not to expose them to war. He knew that would possibly make them think twice about leaving Egypt. So he led them the long way out. They had everything they needed to tackle the journey.

- Broad application: Know what others can handle.
- Your application:

_____

_____

_____

_____

_____

_____

_____

_____

_____

_____

_____

_____

_____

_____

_____

AUGUST 28:

(T) Romans 12:2 (Do not be conformed to this world, but be transformed by the renewal of your mind, that by testing you may discern the will of God, what is good and acceptable and perfect.) We should not think and act like most people in the world. We should challenge our decisions to see if they are based on God's Word. By doing so, we can align our hearts and minds with His will, not our own. We will know what is good and acceptable in His sight.

- Broad application: Be transformed through His Word.
- Your application:

_____

_____

_____

_____

_____

_____

_____

_____

_____

_____

_____

_____

_____

_____

_____

_____

_____

AUGUST 29:

(F) 1 Timothy 6:12 (Fight the good fight of the faith. Take hold of the eternal life to which God called you and about which you made the good confession in the presence of many witnesses.) We will struggle with the daily temptations of sin and the trials of leading a Christian life. It is a real fight, but a good fight. It is good because Jesus has already paved the way. We must cling to what we have already con-fessed as accurate.

- Broad application: Hold on.
- Your application:

_____
_____
_____
_____
_____
_____
_____
_____
_____
_____
_____
_____
_____
_____
_____
_____
_____

AUGUST 30:

(L) Genesis 1:27-28 (So God created man in his image, in the image of God he created him; male and female he created them. And God blessed them. And God said to them, "Be fruitful and multiply and fill the earth and subdue it, and have dominion over the fish of the sea and the birds of the heavens and over every living thing that moves on the planet.") God created us in His image. What an honor! He has given us everything we need to survive and be successful. He also thought enough of us to leave us in charge of all He had created. What a blessing!

- Broad application: Handle your business.
- Your application:

_____
_____
_____
_____
_____
_____
_____
_____
_____
_____
_____
_____
_____
_____
_____
_____

AUGUST 31:

(GE) Romans 11:22 (Note then the kindness and severity of God: severity toward those who have fallen, but God's gentleness to you, provided you continue in his service. Otherwise you will be cut off too.) God can be kind yet severe when needed. He can be harsh to those who show no faith in Him and kind to those who do. God will always show kindness to those who continue to believe and follow Him. But He will turn His back on anyone who chooses to continue to turn their back on Him.

- Broad application: Stay connected.
- Your application:

September 1:

(GO) Psalm 116:12 (What shall I render to the Lord for all his benefits to me?) We will confess our sins and turn from our evil ways. We will publicly proclaim Jesus Christ as our Lord and Savior. We will forever praise His holy name. We will serve Him until we die.

- Broad application: Give Him your life.
- Your application:

_____
_____
_____
_____
_____
_____
_____
_____
_____
_____
_____
_____
_____
_____
_____
_____
_____
_____
_____
_____
_____
_____

September 2:

(J) Psalm 126:5-6 (Those who sow in tears shall reap with shouts of joy! He who goes out weeping, bearing the seed for sowing, shall come home with shouts of joy, bringing his sheaves with him.) It is only momentary when we show signs of stress and despair during hard times. We will shout joy when we make it to the other side. What we gain will be far greater than we could have imagined. We will appreciate our blessings even more. The Lord will restore our lives.

- Broad application: Look forward to the harvest.
- Your application:

_____

_____

_____

_____

_____

_____

_____

_____

_____

_____

_____

_____

_____

_____

_____

_____

_____

September 3:

(LS) 2 Timothy 3:12-13 (Indeed, all who desire to live a godly life in Christ Jesus will get persecuted, while evil people and impostors will go on from bad to worse, deceiving and getting deceived.) Jesus suffered. So it is certain those who want to follow the Lord will also suffer and sacrifice. But it will only be for a while. However, those who practice evil will never be free from deception and corruption. Life will only get worse for them, never better.

- Broad application: Be prepared. Trouble will come.
- Your application:

_____
_____
_____
_____
_____
_____
_____
_____
_____
_____
_____
_____
_____
_____
_____
_____
_____
_____
_____

September 4:

(M) Matthew 11:29 ("Take my yoke upon you, and learn from me, for I am gentle and lowly in heart, and you will find rest for your souls.") To take on the yoke of Jesus is a blessing. As we learn from Him, we find rest in Him. It is like having the most muscular man on your team. He takes up the slack where we will forever fall short.

- Broad application: Be yoked with Jesus.
- Your application:

_____
_____
_____
_____
_____
_____
_____
_____
_____
_____
_____
_____
_____
_____
_____
_____
_____
_____
_____

September 5:

(L) 1 Thessalonians 3:12-13 (And may the Lord make you increase and abound in love for one another, as we do for you, so that he may establish your hearts blameless in holiness before our God and Father, at the coming of our Lord Jesus with all his saints.) Paul's prayer for the church at Thessalonica is to love one another. He hopes the Lord makes their love for each other increase and overflow to everyone. Then the Lord can stand before His Father with proof of their holiness. When He comes back, and all the saints gather, He can be proud of them. He can be proud of us.

- Broad application: Pray for abundant love.
- Your application:

_____
_____
_____
_____
_____
_____
_____
_____
_____
_____
_____
_____
_____
_____
_____
_____

September 6:

(J) Psalm 145:4-5 (One generation shall commend your works to another and declare your mighty acts. On the glorious splendor of your majesty, and on your wondrous works, I will meditate.) The Lord is magnificent! He is gracious, merciful, and kind! We will sing His praises to our children and to everyone who will listen. We will tell them about His mighty acts and the great things He has done in our lives. We will take pleasure in lifting His holy name!

- Broad application: Spread the Word.
- Your application:

_____
_____
_____
_____
_____
_____
_____
_____
_____
_____
_____
_____
_____
_____
_____
_____
_____
_____

SEPTEMBER 7:

(T) 1 Corinthians 7:9 (But if they cannot exercise self-control, they should marry. For it is better to wed than to burn with passion.) The Lord warns us against sexual immorality. We are not of this world. Marriage should be the option if we are in a committed relationship where it becomes increasingly complex to exercise self-control. It would be better to marry than to allow our desires to consume us.

- Broad application: Pray and seek God's way.
- Your application:

_____
_____
_____
_____
_____
_____
_____
_____
_____
_____
_____
_____
_____
_____
_____
_____
_____
_____
_____
_____

September 8:

(L) John 13:34-35 ("A new commandment I give to you is that you love one another: just as I have loved you, you are also to love one another. By this, all people will know that you are my disciples if you show love for one another.") Of course, Jesus is not saying this is a new commandment; He has been teaching love all along. He is just reiterating that to love one another is the ultimate commandment. Jesus is on His way to the cross and will not physically be with His disciples as before. For them to survive and thrive, He wants them to follow the example of His love for them and humanity. He also wants them to know that everyone will still know they belong to Him through their display of love for each other.

- Broad application: Show who you belong to.
- Your application:

_____

_____

_____

_____

_____

_____

_____

_____

_____

_____

_____

_____

September 9:

(F) John 14:6 (Jesus said to him, "I am the way, and the truth, and the life. No one comes to the Father except through me.") We cannot get to God the Father by any other means except through Jesus. It is non-negotiable. The only hope for eternal life is through Jesus. Any other way would mean his death was in vain.

- Broad application: Trust and believe!
- Your application:

_____
_____
_____
_____
_____
_____
_____
_____
_____
_____
_____
_____
_____
_____
_____
_____
_____
_____
_____
_____

SEPTEMBER 10:

(GE) Mark 8:2-3 ("I have compassion for the crowd because they have been with me for three days and have nothing to eat. And if I send them away hungry to their homes, they will faint on the way. And some of them have come from far away.") Jesus cares about His followers. He pays attention to their physical needs as well as their spiritual needs. On this particular day, He did not want them to become faint from hunger on their way home. Some had traveled quite far. So He prepared a meal that fed thousands!

- Broad application: Meet someone's immediate need.
- Your application:

_____

_____

_____

_____

_____

_____

_____

_____

_____

_____

_____

_____

_____

_____

_____

_____

_____

September 11:

(GO) Acts 14:17 (He did not leave himself without witness, for he did well by giving you rains from heaven and fruitful seasons, satisfying your hearts with food and gladness.) God made sure He did well by us. All may not know what is in His Word, but all will see Him in what He has created. We can see Him in the rain He provides and the crops they help produce. Our hearts are glad because of His goodness.

- Broad application: Tell others of His goodness.
- Your application:

_____

_____

_____

_____

_____

_____

_____

_____

_____

_____

_____

_____

_____

_____

_____

_____

_____

_____

September 12:

(J) Proverbs 23:15-16 (My son, if your heart is wise, my heart too will be glad. My inmost being will exult when your lips speak what is right.) Wisdom brings us joy. So God also rejoices when we have insight. He delights when we seek His knowledge in our lives because it leads us to do His will. His wisdom tells us when our actions are correct. His wisdom instructs us to speak what is right.

- Broad application: Make wise decisions.
- Your application:

_____
_____
_____
_____
_____
_____
_____
_____
_____
_____
_____
_____
_____
_____
_____
_____
_____
_____

September 13:

(LS) Luke 14:26-27 ("If anyone comes to me and does not hate his father and mother and wife and children and brothers and sisters, yes, and even his own life, he cannot be my disciple. Whoever does not bear his cross and come after me cannot be my disciple.") To honestly know the Lord, we must know He is not advocating hatred here. He is a God of love. He says we cannot follow Him if He does not come first. Our families and ourselves are secondary. And in doing so, it is a cost we must be willing to pay.

- Broad application: Make Him your priority.
- Your application:

_____

_____

_____

_____

_____

_____

_____

_____

_____

_____

_____

_____

_____

_____

_____

_____

_____

_____

September 14:

(L) 1 Timothy 1:15-16 (The saying is trustworthy and deserving of full acceptance, that Christ Jesus came into the world to save sinners, of whom I am foremost. But I received mercy for this reason, that in me, as the worst, Jesus Christ might display his perfect patience as an example to those who were to believe in him for eternal life.) The Gospel truth is that Jesus came into this world to save sinners. And Paul was the worst of sinners. But Jesus showed mercy on him. He used Paul as an example to others of the absolute patience He would give any sinner if they would believe. Jesus's love is more than capable of saving anyone.

- Broad application: Tell others about Paul.
- Your application:

_____

_____

_____

_____

_____

_____

_____

_____

_____

_____

_____

_____

_____

_____

September 15:

(M) Proverbs 13:10 (By insolence comes nothing but strife, but with those who take advice is wisdom.) Our pride can get us in trouble. It can cause us to have heated disputes. But we can avoid conflict when we humble ourselves and seek God's counsel. God's wisdom then guides us in the right direction.

- Broad application: Be humble and receive wisdom.
- Your application:

_____

_____

_____

_____

_____

_____

_____

_____

_____

_____

_____

_____

_____

_____

_____

_____

_____

_____

_____

_____

September 16:

(P) Judges 18:6 (And the priest said to them, "Go in peace. The journey on which you go is under the eye of the Lord.") It is vital to know God goes before us. It is comforting. Knowing we are in sync with Him gives us peace. It is good to know He is standing watch.

- Broad application: Trust your guide.
- Your application:

_____

_____

_____

_____

_____

_____

_____

_____

_____

_____

_____

_____

_____

_____

_____

_____

_____

_____

_____

_____

SEPTEMBER 17:

(T) 1 John 4:1 (Beloved, do not believe every spirit, but test the spirits to see whether they are from God, for many false prophets have gone out into the world.) There are still many false prophets, even today. So we should be quick to believe only some spirits. We should test them according to their belief in Jesus's death, burial, and resurrection. We should try them according to the fruit of the Spirit.

- Broad application: Study for the tests.
- Your application:

_____

_____

_____

_____

_____

_____

_____

_____

_____

_____

_____

_____

_____

_____

_____

_____

_____

_____

_____

SEPTEMBER 18:

(L) James 2:8-9 (If you fulfill the royal law according to the Scripture, "You shall love your neighbor as yourself," you are doing well. But if you show partiality, you are sinning and are convicted by the law as transgressors.) Once again, love is vital. We know because love covers all, and all are worthy of love. We show confidence in God's love when we love others. If we fulfill God's law to love our neighbor as ourselves, we are doing well. But if we are biased with our love, we sin and fail God.

- Broad application: Practice actual impartiality.
- Your application:

_____

_____

_____

_____

_____

_____

_____

_____

_____

_____

_____

_____

_____

_____

_____

_____

_____

SEPTEMBER 19:

(F) 2 Timothy 4:7-8 (I have fought the good fight, finished the race, and kept my faith. And there is a crown of righteousness that the Lord will give. It is waiting for me and others who have longed for His return.) I have fought the good fight, finished the race, and kept my faith. These words are something every Christian wants to proclaim on that great day. Every one of us wants God's just rewards. But not just for us, for all the saints. We all want to be in that number.

- Broad application: Keep on fighting.
- Your application:

_____

_____

_____

_____

_____

_____

_____

_____

_____

_____

_____

_____

_____

_____

_____

_____

_____

_____

_____

SEPTEMBER 20:

(GE) Joshua 2:12-13 (Now then, please swear to me by the Lord that, as I have dealt kindly with you, you also will deal kindly with my father's house, and give me a sure sign that you will save alive my father and mother, my brothers and sisters, and all who belong to them, and deliver our lives from death.) Rahab hid the spies Joshua had sent to Jericho. She saved their lives. Rahab believed that the God they served was the only true God. So she knew she and her family could find safety in Him when Jericho got destroyed. She knew her kindness would not go unrewarded.

- Broad application: One kind act deserves another.
- Your application:

_____

_____

_____

_____

_____

_____

_____

_____

_____

_____

_____

_____

_____

_____

September 21:

(GO) James 2:16 (And one of you says to them, "Go in peace, be warmed and filled," without giving them the things needed for the body, what good is that?) If someone needs clothes and food, words are useless. Wishing them well and praying for them is not meeting their immediate needs. It is an opportunity for us to show them the goodness of the Lord. It is a chance to do something.

- Broad application: Act!
- Your application:

_____

_____

_____

_____

_____

_____

_____

_____

_____

_____

_____

_____

_____

_____

_____

_____

_____

_____

_____

September 22:

(L) Proverbs 3:9-10 (Honor the Lord with your wealth and with the first fruits of all your produce; then your barns will be filled with plenty, and your vats will be bursting with wine.) Our Father sent His very best when He sent His Son Jesus. So He expects no less from us. We honor Him when we give our tithes and offering. We praise Him when we give our best to others. In doing so, we get back more than we can handle.

- Broad application: Give nothing but the best.
- Your application:

_____

_____

_____

_____

_____

_____

_____

_____

_____

_____

_____

_____

_____

_____

_____

_____

_____

September 23:

(LS) Psalm 119:71 (It is suitable for me that I suffered, that I might learn your statutes.) Life is full of learning experiences. Sacrifices are no exceptions. Anything that leads us to salvation is beneficial. Blessings in disguise are real.

- Broad application: Look for God's lessons.
- Your application:

_____

_____

_____

_____

_____

_____

_____

_____

_____

_____

_____

_____

_____

_____

_____

_____

_____

_____

_____

_____

_____

September 24:

(L) Romans 12:20-21 (To the contrary, "if your enemy is hungry, feed him; if he is thirsty, give him something to drink; for by so doing you will heap burning coals on his head." Do not be overcome by evil, but overcome evil with good.) If our enemy is hungry, give him food. If he is thirsty, give him something to drink. Acts of love should humiliate him for doing evil and may lead him to repent. God is always looking to save souls! Glorify Him by choosing what is good and righteous.

- Broad application: Choose love. Shame the devil.
- Your application:

_____

_____

_____

_____

_____

_____

_____

_____

_____

_____

_____

_____

_____

_____

_____

_____

_____

_____

SEPTEMBER 25:

(M) Romans 12:3 (For by the grace given to me I say to everyone among you not to think of himself more highly than he ought to think, but to think with sober judgment, each according to the measure of faith that God has assigned.) We know we are all significant in God's sight and service. But it should be clear that we still need to submit to Him for our gifts to be revealed. And in exercising those gifts, we are given a measure of faith. Everyone has a role and a purpose.

- Broad application: Surrender to see your gifts.
- Your application:

_____

_____

_____

_____

_____

_____

_____

_____

_____

_____

_____

_____

_____

_____

_____

_____

_____

_____

September 26:

(P) Romans 16:20 (The God of peace will soon crush Satan under your feet. The grace of our Lord Jesus Christ be with you.) Jesus came to set us free from the devil. He came to set us free from sin. Satan will finally be in the lake of fire. Peace will forever reign when He returns.

- Broad application: Know He is coming back.
- Your application:

_____

_____

_____

_____

_____

_____

_____

_____

_____

_____

_____

_____

_____

_____

_____

_____

_____

_____

_____

SEPTEMBER 27:

(T) 1 Peter 4:7 (The end of all things is at hand; therefore, be self-controlled and sober-minded for the sake of your prayers.) Time is winding down. So we should be laser-focused on the Lord. We should be of sound mind and judgment when carrying out His will. Our prayers should be in line with His purpose.

- Broad application: Pray and act accordingly.
- Your application:

_____
_____
_____
_____
_____
_____
_____
_____
_____
_____
_____
_____
_____
_____
_____
_____
_____
_____
_____

September 28:

(F) 1 Chronicles 17:26-27 (And now, O Lord, you are God, and you have promised this good thing to your servant. Now you have been pleased to bless your servant's house, that it may continue forever before you, for it is you, O Lord, who have blessed, and it is blessed forever.) God delights in keeping His promise. He has promised to bless those who obey Him. And this is not a one-time blessing. Everything we have or will ever hope to have is because of Him.

- Broad application: Expect to be blessed.
- Your application:

_____

_____

_____

_____

_____

_____

_____

_____

_____

_____

_____

_____

_____

_____

_____

_____

_____

_____

September 29:

(F) 1 John 5:13-14 (I write these things to you who believe in the name of the Son of God, that you may know that you have eternal life. And this is the confidence we have toward him, that if we ask anything according to his will, he hears us.) There is something about the name Jesus! If we believe, there is enough power in His name to grant eternal life. We have His guarantee on this. And knowing this, we can also be sure He hears our prayers. He answers all of them according to His will.

- Broad application: Ask accordingly.
- Your application:

_____
_____
_____
_____
_____
_____
_____
_____
_____
_____
_____
_____
_____
_____
_____
_____

September 30:

(GE) Matthew 18:21-22 (Peter came up and said, "Lord, how often will my brother sin against me, and I forgive him? As many as seven times?" Jesus said to him, "I do not say to you seven times, but seventy times seven.") We may wonder, "What's the limit to forgiveness?" Sometimes it may seem as if we are constantly turning the other cheek. But Jesus does this for us all day, every day. We count on His grace and mercy toward us. He expects us to extend that same grace and mercy to others.

- Broad application: Think no limit.
- Your application:

_____

_____

_____

_____

_____

_____

_____

_____

_____

_____

_____

_____

_____

_____

_____

_____

_____

October 1:

(GO) Ephesians 4:29 (Let no corrupting talk come out of your mouths, but only such as is suitable for building up, as fits the occasion, that it may give grace to those who hear.) Words are powerful. Any language used to dishonor or tear someone down is not pleasing to God. We should only use uplifting words. In doing so, we spread kindness and goodwill.

- Broad application: Speak to uplift.
- Your application:

_____
_____
_____
_____
_____
_____
_____
_____
_____
_____
_____
_____
_____
_____
_____
_____
_____
_____
_____
_____

OCTOBER 2:

(J) Proverbs 17:22 (A joyful heart is a good medicine, but a crushed spirit dries up the bones.) A cheerful heart can heal the body, mind, and soul. But a broken spirit leads to discouragement and despair. Knowing the Lord can help us keep a cheerful outlook on life. Knowing Him can be encouraging during difficult times.

- Broad application: Take your medicine.
- Your application:

_____

_____

_____

_____

_____

_____

_____

_____

_____

_____

_____

_____

_____

_____

_____

_____

_____

_____

_____

October 3:

(LS) Ecclesiastes 7:8 (Better is the end of a thing than its beginning, and the patient in spirit is better than the proud in spirit.) It is good to finish well. So it is good to have endurance. Pride will never get us to the finish line. We want to hear God say well done.

- Broad application: Play a better second half.
- Your application:

_____

_____

_____

_____

_____

_____

_____

_____

_____

_____

_____

_____

_____

_____

_____

_____

_____

_____

_____

OCTOBER 4:

(L) Matthew 5:44-45 ("But I say to you, Love your enemies and pray for those who persecute you, so that you may be sons of your Father who is in heaven. He makes his sun rise on the evil and good and sends rain on the just and the unjust.") Grace saves us. And that grace is because of God's love for us while we were yet His "enemy." He shows love by giving life-sustaining sun and rain to the just and the unjust. We should follow our Father's lead. We must show the same passion and care toward those we consider our enemies.

- Broad application: Love equally.
- Your application:

_____
_____
_____
_____
_____
_____
_____
_____
_____
_____
_____
_____
_____
_____
_____
_____
_____
_____

OCTOBER 5:

(M) Proverbs 24:17-18 (Do not rejoice when your enemy falls, and let not your heart be glad when he stumbles, lest the Lord see it and be displeased, and turn away his anger from him.) It is not a good look when we are happy due to our enemy's sins or failures. And we should certainly not wish harm on anyone. God knows and sees everything. He will not be pleased. His wrath may turn toward us.

- Broad application: Think but for God's grace...
- Your application:

_____
_____
_____
_____
_____
_____
_____
_____
_____
_____
_____
_____
_____
_____
_____
_____
_____
_____
_____

OCTOBER 6:

(P) Mark 9:50 ("Salt is good, but if the salt has lost its saltiness, how will you make it salty again? Have salt in yourselves, and be at peace with one another.") Salt is good. It is there to improve and influence. Jesus said we are to be the salt of the earth. Through Him, we can be the salt that keeps the peace.

- Broad application: Sprinkle your salt.
- Your application:

_____

_____

_____

_____

_____

_____

_____

_____

_____

_____

_____

_____

_____

_____

_____

_____

_____

_____

_____

OCTOBER 7:

(T) Proverbs 16:23 (The heart of the wise makes his speech judicious and adds persuasiveness to his lips.) We can rely on God's wisdom when we speak. It will lead us to use good judgment. We can then know what to say, how to say it, and to whom. We can be compelling vessels for the Lord.

- Broad application: Use God's wisdom.
- Your application:

_____

_____

_____

_____

_____

_____

_____

_____

_____

_____

_____

_____

_____

_____

_____

_____

_____

_____

_____

_____

OCTOBER 8:

(F) Daniel 3:17-18 (If this is so, our God whom we serve can deliver us from the burning fiery furnace, and he will have us out of your hand, O king. But if not, be it known to you, O king, that we will not serve your gods or worship the golden image you have set up.) Shadrach, Meshach, and Abednego surely knew the God they worshipped! They knew He could deliver them from any situation that would have caused them to get hurt or harmed. But they also knew it had to be within His will. So they told King Nebuchadnezzar that whatever God's will would be, it still would not sway their faith or their decision. They would never serve the king's gods or worship any golden images.

- Broad application: Serve only Him.
- Your application:

_____

_____

_____

_____

_____

_____

_____

_____

_____

_____

_____

_____

_____

OCTOBER 9:

(F) Exodus 14:13-14 (And Moses said to the people, "Fear not, stand firm, and see the salvation of the Lord, which he will work for you today. For the Egyptians whom you see today, you shall never see again. The Lord will fight for you, and you have only to be silent.) The Egyptians were in hot pursuit of the Israelites. It seemed as if they had them trapped at the Red Sea. The Israelites seemed to believe the same. But Moses told them not to be afraid, to stand firm, hold their peace, and behold God's salvation. The Lord was going to deliver them once and for all.

- Broad application: Sit back and allow God...
- Your application:

_____
_____
_____
_____
_____
_____
_____
_____
_____
_____
_____
_____
_____
_____
_____
_____
_____

OCTOBER 10:

(GE) Luke 14:13-14 ("When you give a feast, invite the poor, the crippled, the lame, the blind. God will bless you because they cannot repay you. For you will be repaid at the resurrection of the just.") When we follow the Lord, it may put us outside our comfort zone. In this example, Jesus urges us to go beyond the familiar. He suggests we extend an invitation to those genuinely in need because they are less likely to be able to repay us. We should not be selfish or selective in our acts of kindness because we might miss an opportunity to serve and witness. It is a blessing to help anyone.

- Broad application: Invite everyone to the table.
- Your application:

_____

_____

_____

_____

_____

_____

_____

_____

_____

_____

_____

_____

_____

_____

_____

_____

OCTOBER 11:

(GO) Deuteronomy 6:18 (And you shall do what is right and good in the sight of the Lord, that it may go well with you, and that you may go in and take possession of the good land that the Lord swore to give to your fathers.) Do what is proper and sound according to the Lord. He will be pleased. In doing so, God will grant us access to all He has that is good. What He did for our ancestors, He will do for us.

- Broad application: Discover God's goodness.
- Your application:

_____

_____

_____

_____

_____

_____

_____

_____

_____

_____

_____

_____

_____

_____

_____

_____

_____

_____

_____

OCTOBER 12:

(J) Psalm 119:14 (In the way of your testimonies I delight as much as in all riches.) God is! He is whoever and whatever we need Him to be. He is our Redeemer! The joy of knowing Him is priceless!

- Broad application: Delight in who He is.
- Your application:

_____

_____

_____

_____

_____

_____

_____

_____

_____

_____

_____

_____

_____

_____

_____

_____

_____

_____

_____

_____

_____

_____

OCTOBER 13:

(LS) 1 Thessalonians 5:14 (And we urge you, brothers, admonish the idle, encourage the fainthearted, help the weak, be patient with them all.) Christians are encouraged to counsel those who are rowdy or unruly. We should support those who lack courage or clear direction. We should help those who are weak or flawed. But we must remember that patience is needed to tackle all these things.

- Broad application: Roll up your sleeves.
- Your application:

_____
_____
_____
_____
_____
_____
_____
_____
_____
_____
_____
_____
_____
_____
_____
_____
_____
_____

OCTOBER 14:

(L) Luke 10:34-35 ("He went to him and bound up his wounds, pouring on oil and wine. Then he set him on his animal, brought him to an inn, and cared for him. And the next day, he took out two denari and gave them to the innkeeper, saying, 'Take care of him, and whatever more you spend, I will repay you when I come back.'") Wow, the good Samaritan parable! What an example! We should all have stories like this. We should all be able to glorify and uplift the name of the Lord in such a pleasant way. We can certainly find enough opportunities to do so.

- Broad application: Work on your Christian resume.
- Your application:

_____
_____
_____
_____
_____
_____
_____
_____
_____
_____
_____
_____
_____
_____
_____

October 15:

(M) 1 Peter 3:15-16 (But in your hearts revere Christ as Lord. Always be prepared to answer everyone who asks you to give the reason for your hope. But do this with gentleness and respect, keeping a clear conscience, so that those who speak maliciously against your good behavior in Christ may be ashamed of their slander.) Our God is holy. And we should always be ready to state our case as to why we believe in Him. But we should do this with humility and respect. In doing so, those who speak evil of us will not benefit from their actions. Our behavior is our most incredible testimony.

- Broad application: Cause a scandal. Be meek.
- Your application:

_____

_____

_____

_____

_____

_____

_____

_____

_____

_____

_____

_____

_____

_____

_____

OCTOBER 16:

(P) Proverbs 16:7 (When a man's ways please the Lord, he makes even his enemies be at peace with him.) The Lord is pleased when we allow Him to order our steps. We, in turn, are blessed with peace. We can feel that peace in every aspect of our lives. God can even make our enemies reconcile with us.

- Broad application: Please Him.
- Your application:

_____

_____

_____

_____

_____

_____

_____

_____

_____

_____

_____

_____

_____

_____

_____

_____

_____

_____

_____

OCTOBER 17:

(T) Romans 6:12 (Let not sin therefore reign in your mortal body, to make you obey its passions.) Actual self-control is through the help of the Holy Spirit. It is the only way sin does not become a way of life. Giving up and giving in to temptation is not inevitable just because we are human. We do not have to allow sin to rule our lives.

- Broad application: Yield not to temptation.
- Your application:

_____

_____

_____

_____

_____

_____

_____

_____

_____

_____

_____

_____

_____

_____

_____

_____

_____

_____

_____

_____

OCTOBER 18:

(F) Mark 10:26-27 (And they were exceedingly astonished, and said to him, "Then who can be saved?" Jesus looked at them and said, "With man it is impossible, but not with God. For all things are possible with God.") No, we cannot save ourselves. The world will tell us we can do just about anything. But we know who has saving power! Jesus is the only one with this unique capability. Only through faith in Him is salvation possible.

- Broad application: Don't look to man.
- Your application:

_____
_____
_____
_____
_____
_____
_____
_____
_____
_____
_____
_____
_____
_____
_____
_____
_____

OCTOBER 19:

(F) Luke 4:7-8 (If you, then, will worship me, it will all be yours. And Jesus answered him, "It says, You shall worship the Lord your God, and him only shall you serve.") Yes, the devil had the nerve to try and tempt Jesus! But the devil had nothing to offer Jesus. Jesus in the flesh still knew what a mighty God He chose to serve. He knew there was no one He would care to worship. He knew there was no one He <u>would</u> worship.

- Broad application: Know who holds your future.
- Your application:

_____

_____

_____

_____

_____

_____

_____

_____

_____

_____

_____

_____

_____

_____

_____

_____

_____

_____

OCTOBER 20:

(GO) 1 Timothy 4:4 (God created everything good, so nothing is rejected if we first give thanks.) God is good. Everything created by Him is good. So we should give thanks by showing our acceptance of His goodness. There is always a reason to acknowledge Him.

- Broad application: Give thanks.
- Your application:

_____
_____
_____
_____
_____
_____
_____
_____
_____
_____
_____
_____
_____
_____
_____
_____
_____
_____
_____
_____
_____

OCTOBER 21:

(J) Jeremiah 15:16 (I found your words and ate them. Your words became a joy to me and the delight of my heart. Because of you, I am called by your name, O Lord, God of hosts.) It's pure joy when we discover God's Word. It becomes food for our souls. We can be grateful under any circumstance. We are happy to be called by His name.

- Broad application: Feed on His Word.
- Your application:

_____

_____

_____

_____

_____

_____

_____

_____

_____

_____

_____

_____

_____

_____

_____

_____

_____

_____

OCTOBER 22:

(LS) James 1:4 (And let steadfastness have its full effect, that you may be perfect and complete, lacking in nothing.) Let patience have its full effect. And that effect is perfection, wholeness. But not by the world's definition but by God's. At that point, we should lack nothing needed to grow and thrive in the Lord.

- Broad application: Let patience have its way.
- Your application:

_____

_____

_____

_____

_____

_____

_____

_____

_____

_____

_____

_____

_____

_____

_____

_____

_____

_____

_____

_____

OCTOBER 23:

(L) 2 Corinthians 5:14-15 (For the love of Christ controls us, because we have concluded this: that one has died for all; therefore all have died; and he died for all, that those who live might no longer live for themselves but for him who for their sake died and He rose.) We realize that when Christ died for us, we all died. The Holy Spirit transforms our hearts and minds. This great act of love compels us to become new creatures. And as new creatures, we no longer live for ourselves but for Him. We become His special ambassadors.

- Broad application: Be one with Him.
- Your application:

_____

_____

_____

_____

_____

_____

_____

_____

_____

_____

_____

_____

_____

_____

_____

_____

_____

OCTOBER 24:

(M) Numbers 20:11-12 (Moses lifted his hand and struck the rock with his staff twice; the water came out abundantly, and the congregation drank, along with their livestock. And the Lord said to Moses and Aaron, "Because you did not believe in me, to uphold me as holy in the eyes of the people of Israel, you shall not bring this assembly into the land that I have given them.") God instructed Moses to take the rod, along with Aaron, and gather the congregation of Israel together. God then told Moses to speak to the rock so it would bring forth water for the people and their livestock to drink. But Moses took it upon himself to strike the rock twice with his staff. And because of Moses's disobedience, his actions failed to magnify God's sovereignty and holiness. God denied Moses the privilege of taking the people into the Promised Land.

- Broad application: Follow God's exact instructions.
- Your application:

_____

_____

_____

_____

_____

_____

_____

_____

_____

_____

_____

_____

OCTOBER 25:

(P) Psalm 29:11 (May the Lord give strength to his people and bless his people with peace!) The Lord promises to strengthen His people. The Lord promises to bless His people with peace. He is the only one who has the power to do these things. As His people, we can count on His promises.

- Broad application: Hang on to His promises.
- Your application:

_____

_____

_____

_____

_____

_____

_____

_____

_____

_____

_____

_____

_____

_____

_____

_____

_____

_____

_____

_____

OCTOBER 26:

(T) Proverbs 29:11 (A fool gives full vent to his spirit, but a wise man quickly holds it back.) It is not according to the will of God that we give someone "a piece of our mind." That is foolish talk. That is selfish talk. But an attempt to control our urges is Christ-like.

- Broad application: Know it's not about you.
- Your application:

_____

_____

_____

_____

_____

_____

_____

_____

_____

_____

_____

_____

_____

_____

_____

_____

_____

_____

_____

_____

_____

OCTOBER 27:

(F) Romans 3:22-23 (...the righteousness of God through faith in Jesus Christ for all who believe. For there is no distinction: for all have sinned and fall short of the glory of God.) No one is immune to sin. And because of sin, we will always fall short of God's glory. We cannot achieve righteousness on our own. But we are all made righteous through Jesus Christ. This righteousness is there for all of those who believe.

- Broad application: Count on God's righteousness.
- Your application:

_____

_____

_____

_____

_____

_____

_____

_____

_____

_____

_____

_____

_____

_____

_____

_____

_____

_____

OCTOBER 28:

(F) Psalm 34:9-10 (Oh, fear the Lord, you saints, for those who fear him have no lack! The young lions are weak and hungry; but those who seek the Lord lack no good thing.) All saints fear the Lord. Be in total awe of Him. Those who fear Him reap his goodness. Those who seek Him will not want like others. Those who have faith in Him know He will bless them.

- Broad application: Marvel at His awesomeness.
- Your application:

_____

_____

_____

_____

_____

_____

_____

_____

_____

_____

_____

_____

_____

_____

_____

_____

_____

_____

OCTOBER 29:

(L) Ephesians 5:1-2 (Therefore be imitators of God, as beloved children. And walk in love, as Christ loved us and gave himself up for us, a fragrant offering and sacrifice to God.) As children of God, we want to be more like Him daily. Our desire to be more Christ-like comes from a genuine love for Him. Our hope is not to pay Him back but to be worthy of the sacrifice he made for all of us. Dying for our sins was better than any sweet-smelling sacrifice ever offered in the past. His sacrifice was true love.

- Broad application: Imitate the author of love.
- Your application:

_____

_____

_____

_____

_____

_____

_____

_____

_____

_____

_____

_____

_____

_____

_____

_____

OCTOBER 30:

(J) 1 Chronicles 29:9 (Then the people rejoiced because they had given willingly, for with a whole heart they had offered freely to the Lord. David, the king, also rejoiced greatly.) David gave generously to the building of the temple. He gave his best. Others willingly followed David's example. They all delivered to the Lord with joy in their hearts.

- Broad application: Give your best gifts.
- Your application:

_____

_____

_____

_____

_____

_____

_____

_____

_____

_____

_____

_____

_____

_____

_____

_____

_____

_____

_____

_____

OCTOBER 31:

(LS) James 1:12 (Blessed is the man who remains steadfast under trial, for when he has stood the test, he will receive the crown of life, which God has promised to those who love him.) Our trials can lead to unexpected blessings. Going through can be much more rewarding than going around. On the road to salvation, Christian maturity and patience are priceless. The promise of a crown is waiting for us.

- Broad application: Stay the course.
- Your application:

_____

_____

_____

_____

_____

_____

_____

_____

_____

_____

_____

_____

_____

_____

_____

_____

_____

_____

_____

November 1:

(M) Psalm 119:33-34 (Teach me, O Lord, the way of your statutes; and I will keep it to the end. Give me understanding, that I may keep your law and observe it wholeheartedly.) The psalmist asks God to teach him His ways so he can follow Him until the end of his days. He is asking for understanding to discern God's Word so he can live accordingly. He wants to do this with his whole heart and soul. He is praying for wisdom. He is praying for salvation.

- Broad application: Know who has the answer.
- Your application:

_____

_____

_____

_____

_____

_____

_____

_____

_____

_____

_____

_____

_____

_____

_____

_____

_____

_____

_____

November 2:

(P) Psalm 37:37 (Mark the blameless and behold the upright, for there is a future for the man of peace.) Through Jesus Christ, we are made perfect in His eyes. Through Jesus Christ, we are made righteous. Because of this, people take notice. Because of this, our inner peace shines through.

- Broad application: Be someone to behold.
- Your application:

_____
_____
_____
_____
_____
_____
_____
_____
_____
_____
_____
_____
_____
_____
_____
_____
_____
_____
_____

November 3:

(T) Titus 1:8 (...but hospitable, a lover of good, self-controlled, upright, holy, and disciplined.) We should be friendly and welcoming as witnesses and teachers in or outside the church. We should love what is good. We should practice discipline. We should lead good and holy lives.

- Broad application: Be under God's control.
- Your application:

_____
_____
_____
_____
_____
_____
_____
_____
_____
_____
_____
_____
_____
_____
_____
_____
_____
_____
_____
_____

November 4:

(F) Proverbs 3:7-8 (Be not wise in your own eyes; fear the Lord, and turn away from evil. It will heal your flesh and refresh your bones.) We need so much more than our knowledge in this world. There are things we are just not able to see. But when we trust Jesus, He has supernatural wisdom. It is life-sustaining. It is rejuvenating!

- Broad application: Receive God's wisdom.
- Your application:

_____

_____

_____

_____

_____

_____

_____

_____

_____

_____

_____

_____

_____

_____

_____

_____

_____

_____

November 5:

(F) Job 2:9-10 (His wife said, "Do you still hold your integrity fast? Curse God and die." But he said to her, "You speak as one of the foolish women would speak. Shall we receive good from God, and shall we not receive evil?" In all this, Job did not sin with his lips.) Yes, Job held on to his integrity as well as his faith! There was no need to curse God. He knew God had not left him. Job knew that all things work together for good for those who love the Lord! He held fast to his faith and God's Word.

- Broad application: Hold on for dear life!
- Your application:

_____

_____

_____

_____

_____

_____

_____

_____

_____

_____

_____

_____

_____

_____

_____

_____

_____

November 6:

(GO) Ephesians 5:8-9 (For at one time you were darkness, but now you are light in the Lord. Walk as children of light for the fruit of light is found in all that is good and right and true.) At one time, we were dark because we walked in darkness. Now we are light because we walk in the light. By walking in the Lord, we see the light. We are no longer spiritually ignorant, headed toward damnation. Our fruit is all that is good, righteous, and true.

- Broad application: Shine the light of goodness.
- Your application:

_____
_____
_____
_____
_____
_____
_____
_____
_____
_____
_____
_____
_____
_____
_____
_____
_____
_____

November 7:

(L) 1 Peter 4:8-9 (Above all, keep loving one another earnestly, since love covers a multitude of sins. Show hospitality to one another without grumbling.) God commands this. No matter what, we should be eager to love. We should seek ways to show love to each other daily. It does cover a multitude of sins.

- Broad application: Continue in love.
- Your application:

_____
_____
_____
_____
_____
_____
_____
_____
_____
_____
_____
_____
_____
_____
_____
_____
_____
_____
_____
_____

November 8:

(J) Psalm 71:23-24 (My lips will shout for joy when I sing praises to you; my soul, which you have redeemed. And my tongue will talk of your righteous help all the day long, for they have been put to shame and disappointed who sought to do me hurt.) We shout for joy when we praise the Lord. Our souls rejoice when we think of how He has redeemed us. We want to tell everyone of His goodness. No one can hurt us. His righteousness is forever.

- Broad application: Give all praise unto Him!
- Your application:

_____
_____
_____
_____
_____
_____
_____
_____
_____
_____
_____
_____
_____
_____
_____
_____
_____
_____

November 9:

(LS) Luke 21:19 ("By your endurance, you will gain your lives.") We serve a patient God. We labor for a just God. So through our God-given patience, we will see God's justice. And that justice will be eternal life.

- Broad application: Expect a life sentence.
- Your application:

_____
_____
_____
_____
_____
_____
_____
_____
_____
_____
_____
_____
_____
_____
_____
_____
_____
_____
_____
_____
_____
_____

NOVEMBER 10:

(L) 1 John 3:17-18 (But if anyone has the world's goods and sees his brother in need, yet closes his heart against him, how does he have God's love? Little children, let us not love in word or talk but in deed and truth.) God is always our best example of love. He saw our need for redemption and sent His Son, Jesus Christ, so we could all have access to eternal life. So, just as He addressed our needs, we should do the same for our brothers and sisters. Mature Christians show true love in this manner. Our hearts move us to act, not just give lip service.

- Broad application: Less talk, more action.
- Your application:

_____

_____

_____

_____

_____

_____

_____

_____

_____

_____

_____

_____

_____

_____

_____

_____

_____

_____

November 11:

(M) John 13:14-15 ("If I then, your Lord and Teacher, have washed your feet, you also ought to wash one another's feet. For I have given you an example, that you also should do just as I have done to you.") As a teacher, Jesus was always able to demonstrate to others. On His way to the cross, He washed his disciples' feet. He used this event as one last example of true humility relating to Christian love and service. He wanted them to know that their stature or title didn't matter. The only thing that mattered was their ability to humble themselves.

- Broad application: Be prepared to get dirty.
- Your application:

_____

_____

_____

_____

_____

_____

_____

_____

_____

_____

_____

_____

_____

_____

_____

_____

_____

November 12:

(P) 1 Corinthians 14:33 (For God is not a God of confusion but peace, as in all the churches of the saints.) We know God is not a God of confusion. He is a God of peace. He wants peace to be in our hearts, our homes, and our churches. Those of us in Christ know this.

- Broad application: Practice peace.
- Your application:

_____
_____
_____
_____
_____
_____
_____
_____
_____
_____
_____
_____
_____
_____
_____
_____
_____
_____
_____
_____
_____
_____

November 13:

(T) 1 Peter 1:13 (Therefore, preparing your minds for action, and being sober-minded, set your hope entirely on the grace that God will bring to you at the revelation of Jesus Christ.) Obedience is a process. It requires mental preparation. It requires self-control. It requires believing in the power of God's favor as Jesus Christ reveals Himself to us.

- Broad application: Get ready to act.
- Your application:

_____

_____

_____

_____

_____

_____

_____

_____

_____

_____

_____

_____

_____

_____

_____

_____

_____

_____

_____

_____

November 14:

(F) Psalm 31:1-2 (In you, O Lord, do I take refuge; let me never be put to shame; in your righteousness deliver me! Incline your ear to me; rescue me speedily! Be a rock of refuge for me, a strong fortress to save me!) The Lord is our protector. He is our Deliverer. On these, we can never be ashamed. We know who we can rely on to meet our every need. Let Him be our Rock!

- Broad application: Declare His saving grace!
- Your application:

_____

_____

_____

_____

_____

_____

_____

_____

_____

_____

_____

_____

_____

_____

_____

_____

_____

_____

NOVEMBER 15:

(GO) Psalm 71:15-16 (My mouth will tell of your righteous acts, of your deeds of salvation all the day, for their number is past my knowledge. With the mighty deeds of the Lord God, I will come and remind them of your righteousness, yours alone.) We will want to tell everyone about God's acts of goodness. We will want to tell everyone how He can save souls. We will never be able to proclaim it all because it is impossible to count all His good deeds. But that will not keep us from trying. We will keep reminding others of His righteousness.

- Broad application: Run and tell that!
- Your application:

_____

_____

_____

_____

_____

_____

_____

_____

_____

_____

_____

_____

_____

_____

_____

_____

November 16:

(J) Psalm 103:1-2 (Bless the Lord, O my soul, and all that is within me, bless his holy name! Bless the Lord, O my soul, and forget not all his benefits.) Praise the Lord with everything that is in us. Praise His holy name! Praise the Lord because we can't forget all His benefits. A few are forgiveness, health, grace, mercy, and redemption. Praise Him for everything He has done!

- Broad application: Never forget what He's done.
- Your application:

_____
_____
_____
_____
_____
_____
_____
_____
_____
_____
_____
_____
_____
_____
_____
_____
_____
_____
_____
_____
_____

NOVEMBER 17:

(LS) Isaiah 30:18 (Therefore the Lord waits to be gracious to you, and therefore he exalts himself to show mercy to you. For the Lord is a God of justice; blessed are all those who wait for him.) God yearns to be gracious and merciful to us all. It is <u>who</u> He is. So it is a blessing to wait for Him. His justice is like nothing here on earth.

- Broad application: Be ready to be blessed.
- Your application:

_____
_____
_____
_____
_____
_____
_____
_____
_____
_____
_____
_____
_____
_____
_____
_____
_____
_____
_____
_____

NOVEMBER 18:

(L) Isaiah 54:9-10 ("This is like the days of Noah to me: as I swore that the waters of Noah should no more go over the earth, so I have sworn that I will not be angry with you, and will not rebuke you. For the mountains may depart and the hills go away, but my steadfast love shall not depart from you, and my covenant of peace shall remain," says the Lord, who has compassion on you.) God has promised He will not destroy the earth with water as He did in Noah's day. He will not show that kind of anger toward us or reprimand us in that way again. His love for us will never change. He will never take away His promise of peace. His mercy is forever.

- Broad application: Keep your word.
- Your application:

_____
_____
_____
_____
_____
_____
_____
_____
_____
_____
_____
_____
_____
_____
_____
_____

NOVEMBER 19:

(P) Hebrews 10:30-31 (For we know him who said, "Vengeance is mine; I will repay." And again, "The Lord will judge his people." It is a fearful thing to fall into the hands of the living God.) We know what God says about "paybacks." We should not concern ourselves with these things. We can rest assured that God will handle it because He demands justice. He is a God of judgment as well as grace and mercy. He is a living God!

- Broad application: Leave it to the Lord.
- Your application:

_____
_____
_____
_____
_____
_____
_____
_____
_____
_____
_____
_____
_____
_____
_____
_____
_____
_____

November 20:

(T) Proverbs 9:7-8 (Whoever corrects a scoffer gets himself abuse, and he who reproves a wicked man incurs injury. Do not reprove a scoffer, or he will hate you; reprove a wise man, and he will love you.) Sometimes we may run into those who will try to mock or make fun of our faith in our Lord and Savior, Jesus Christ. When this happens, we should not try to correct them. It will only lead to more ridicule. We cannot reason with the unreasonable. Only the wise are open to constructive criticism.

- Broad application: Pick your battles.
- Your application:

_____
_____
_____
_____
_____
_____
_____
_____
_____
_____
_____
_____
_____
_____
_____
_____
_____
_____

NOVEMBER 21:

(F) Deuteronomy 31:5-6 (And the Lord will give them over to you, and you shall do to them according to the commandment that I have commanded you. Be strong and courageous. Do not fear or be in dread of them, for it is the Lord your God who goes with you. He will not leave you or forsake you.) Just as God was with the Israelites as they headed into the Promised Land, He is with us today as we carry out His ministry. He is right there as we go into the unknown. He will make way for what He has commissioned us to do. There is no need to be afraid. Be strong and know that God will never leave or turn His back on us.

- Broad application: Let God lead the charge.
- Your application:

_____

_____

_____

_____

_____

_____

_____

_____

_____

_____

_____

_____

_____

_____

_____

NOVEMBER 22:

(GO) 1 Samuel 19:4-5 (And Jonathan spoke well of David to Saul, his father, and said, "Let not the king sin against his servant David, because he has not sinned against you, and because his deeds have brought good to you. He took his life in his hand, struck down the Philistine, and the Lord worked a great salvation for all Israel. You saw it and rejoiced. Why then will you sin against innocent blood by killing David without cause?") Jonathan and David were the best of friends. But Saul (Jonathan's father) had the desire to kill David. So Jonathan went to his father on David's behalf. He told him that not only had David not given him any cause to hurt him, but David also risked his life to save Israel. Jonathan wanted his father to see that he would sin against God if he killed David.

- Broad application: Do the right thing regardless.
- Your application:

_____

_____

_____

_____

_____

_____

_____

_____

_____

_____

_____

_____

_____

November 23:

(J) Ecclesiastes 5:18-19 (Behold, what I have seen to be good and fitting is to eat and drink and enjoy all the toil with which one toils under the sun the few days of his life that God has given him, for this is his lot. Everyone also to whom God has given wealth and possessions and power to enjoy them, and to accept his lot and rejoice in his toil—-this is the gift of God.) Whatever time the Lord has blessed us to have, we should find joy in it. We should have a cheerful spirit. And if God has chosen to give us wealth, possessions, and power, we should also rejoice. These gifts are added blessings from God. We should be pleased with whatever liberties God allows us to have.

- Broad application: Be happy with your lot.
- Your application:

_____
_____
_____
_____
_____
_____
_____
_____
_____
_____
_____
_____
_____

November 24:

(LS) Luke 9:24-25 ("For whoever would save his life will lose it, but whoever loses his life for my sake will save it. For what does it profit a man if he gains the whole world and loses or forfeits himself?") When we try to hang on to what this world calls life, we lose our life. But to those in Christ, we must let go to gain true life. We know the sacrifices we make when we follow the Lord are not in vain. We may die in this world. But we know eternal life awaits us.

- Broad application: Live for the Lord!
- Your application:

_____
_____
_____
_____
_____
_____
_____
_____
_____
_____
_____
_____
_____
_____
_____
_____
_____
_____
_____

NOVEMBER 25:

(L) I John 3:11 (This is the message you have heard from the beginning, that we should love one another.) We cannot keep qualifying God's people for God's love. We do not care according to our idea of worthiness. From the beginning, the message has been to love, period! God never changes.

- Broad application: Use His standards, not yours.
- Your application:

_____

_____

_____

_____

_____

_____

_____

_____

_____

_____

_____

_____

_____

_____

_____

_____

_____

_____

_____

_____

NOVEMBER 26:

(P) Hebrews 4:10-11 (For whoever has entered God's rest has also rested from his works as God did from his. Let us, therefore, strive to enter that rest, so that no one may fall by the same sort of disobedience.) Jesus entered into God's rest and now sits at the right hand of the Father. He finished His work as His Father did on the 7th day here on earth. We strive to enter that identical rest here on earth as we work and serve the Lord and ultimately have eternal rest. We don't want to be like those who completely turn away from God. They will never find peace and rest.

- Broad application: Work until called to rest.
- Your application:

_____
_____
_____
_____
_____
_____
_____
_____
_____
_____
_____
_____
_____
_____
_____

NOVEMBER 27:

(T) Proverbs 10:18-19 (The one who conceals hatred has lying lips, and whoever utters slander is a fool. When words are many, transgression is not lacking, but whoever restrains his lips is prudent.) If we openly slander someone, we are crazy. We are foolish if we pretend to be friends through our words yet harbor hatred. We are bound to say something careless or false if we talk too much. These are examples of acting outside of God's will. But if we "bridle our tongue," then we are wise.

- Broad application: Consider who, what, when, where.
- Your application:

_____

_____

_____

_____

_____

_____

_____

_____

_____

_____

_____

_____

_____

_____

_____

_____

_____

NOVEMBER 28:

(F) Psalm 118:5-6 (Out of my distress, I called on the Lord; the Lord answered me and set me free. The Lord is on my side; I will not fear. What can man do to me?) We are so blessed to call on the Lord anytime, anywhere. And we have faith He will answer. When we feel burdened, He can set us free. He is always on our side. There is nothing man can do to us.

- Broad application: Don't worry about man.
- Your application:

_____

_____

_____

_____

_____

_____

_____

_____

_____

_____

_____

_____

_____

_____

_____

_____

_____

_____

NOVEMBER 29:

(GO) Proverbs 24:1-2 (Be not envious of evil men, nor desire to be with them, for their hearts devise violence, and their lips talk of trouble.) Sometimes we may find ourselves being envious of others. We may resent not being able to participate in wrongdoing. But when we think about it, their actions only lead to death and destruction. Their behavior is of the devil and offensive to the Lord. Displaying God's goodness is the only safe option.

- Broad application: Stay away from trouble.
- Your application:

_____

_____

_____

_____

_____

_____

_____

_____

_____

_____

_____

_____

_____

_____

_____

_____

_____

_____

NOVEMBER 30:

(J) Psalm 136:1-2 (Give thanks to the Lord, for he is good, for his steadfast love endures forever. Give thanks to the God of gods, for his steadfast love endures forever.) Praise the Lord because He is good. His passion and mercy will last forever! Praise the one and only true God. His love and compassion will last forever! He is so worthy of being praised!

- Broad application: Know who truly loves you!
- Your application:

_____

_____

_____

_____

_____

_____

_____

_____

_____

_____

_____

_____

_____

_____

_____

_____

_____

_____

_____

_____

_____

DECEMBER 1:

(LS) Psalm 25:4-5 (Make me know your ways, O Lord; teach me your paths. Lead me in your truth and teach me, for you are the God of my salvation; for you, I wait all the day long.) The Lord is here to teach us. He is here to lead us. He is the God of our salvation. But we must wait on Him to be taught, shown, and saved. We must be patient.

- Broad application: Be a good student.
- Your application:

_____
_____
_____
_____
_____
_____
_____
_____
_____
_____
_____
_____
_____
_____
_____
_____
_____
_____
_____
_____
_____

DECEMBER 2:

(L) Matthew 5:48 ("You must be perfect, as your heavenly Father is perfect.") Perfection is paramount with all the fruit of the Spirit. It simply means daily sanctification with the help of the Holy Spirit and modeling the example Jesus set for us. So in the case of love, we must love as Jesus loves. His perfect love (agape love) is complete because He shows love and mercy to all.

- Broad application: Strive for perfection.
- Your application:

_____

_____

_____

_____

_____

_____

_____

_____

_____

_____

_____

_____

_____

_____

_____

_____

_____

_____

_____

December 3:

(T) 1 Peter 1:14-15 (As obedient children, do not be conformed to the passions of your former ignorance, but as he who called you is holy, you also be holy in all your conduct.) We are children of God. We walk in His light. We are obedient to His will, not our own. And as such, we can't afford to return to our former way of living. Our behavior reflects our dedication to God.

- Broad application: Don't act ignorant.
- Your application:

_____

_____

_____

_____

_____

_____

_____

_____

_____

_____

_____

_____

_____

_____

_____

_____

_____

_____

_____

DECEMBER 4:

(F) John 14:1-2 ("Let not your hearts be troubled. Trust in God; also believe in me. In my Father's house are many rooms. If it were not so, would I have told you that I go to prepare a place for you?") Jesus is telling His disciples not to worry. If they believe in God, they should have faith in Him too. He tells them His Father's house has enough room for all of them. So He is going to get things ready for them. But He has to leave for a while to do so.

- Broad application: Believe in Jesus's arrangements.
- Your application:

_____

_____

_____

_____

_____

_____

_____

_____

_____

_____

_____

_____

_____

_____

_____

_____

_____

_____

_____

December 5:

(GO) Proverbs 3:27-28 (Do not withhold good from those to whom it is due, when it is in your power to do it. Do not say to your neighbor, "Go, and come again, tomorrow I will give it"—-when you have it with you.) Tomorrow is not a promise. Therefore, we should "seize the day!" God blesses us so we can help others. When given a chance to make a difference in someone's life, do it then. Please do not put them off.

- Broad application: Do good while you can.
- Your application:

_____

_____

_____

_____

_____

_____

_____

_____

_____

_____

_____

_____

_____

_____

_____

_____

_____

_____

December 6:

(J) Psalm 33:20-21 (Our soul waits for the Lord; he is our help and shield, for our heart is glad in him because we trust in his holy name.) We know to call on the name of Jesus. We know who to go to for help and protection. We know we can count on Him like no other. It brings us joy to know He is there for us. We trust in His holy name.

- Broad application: Trust Him to be there.
- Your application:

_____

_____

_____

_____

_____

_____

_____

_____

_____

_____

_____

_____

_____

_____

_____

_____

_____

_____

_____

_____

December 7:

(L) 1 John 2:1-2 (My little children, I am writing these things to you so that you may not sin. But if anyone does sin, we have an advocate with the Father, Jesus Christ the righteous. He is the propitiation for our sins, not only for ours but also for the whole world's sins.) Our goal in life is to overcome evil and to be more Christ-like with the help of the Holy Spirit. We should take on a daily process of sanctification. But we know we have Jesus Christ as our advocate when we sin. He is the one who stepped in as a willing sacrifice for all of our sins. And because of these loving acts, He is the solution for the whole world.

- Broad application: Share this information with others.
- Your application:

_____

_____

_____

_____

_____

_____

_____

_____

_____

_____

_____

_____

_____

_____

_____

_____

December 8:

(F) Romans 1:12 (That is, we may be mutually encouraged by each other's faith, both yours and mine.) This Christian journey is a personal, individualized one. But it also requires interaction with others. We are to serve one another. We are to encourage one another's faith.

- Broad application: Support each other.
- Your application:

_____

_____

_____

_____

_____

_____

_____

_____

_____

_____

_____

_____

_____

_____

_____

_____

_____

_____

_____

_____

_____

_____

December 9:

(F) Habakkuk 2:4 ("Behold, his soul is puffed up; it is not upright within him, but the righteous shall live by his faith.) Arrogance and pride are not traits of the righteous. These traits are associated with those who are lost. Characteristics of the righteous are modesty and humility. They live by their faith in God.

- Broad application: Set aside pride.
- Your application:

_____

_____

_____

_____

_____

_____

_____

_____

_____

_____

_____

_____

_____

_____

_____

_____

_____

_____

_____

_____

December 10:

(T) James 4:7-8 (Submit yourselves therefore to God. Resist the devil, and he will flee from you. Draw near to God, and he will draw near to you. Cleanse your hands, sinners, and purify your hearts, you double-minded.) We should submit ourselves to God. He is the only one who can lead us into battle against the devil. When we draw close to Him, He draws close to us. Through Him, we learn to do good deeds. Through Him, we are taught to have pure hearts.

- Broad application: Lean and depend on God.
- Your application:

_____

_____

_____

_____

_____

_____

_____

_____

_____

_____

_____

_____

_____

_____

_____

_____

_____

December 11:

(F) Psalm 46:1-2 (God is our refuge and strength, a delightful help in trouble. Therefore, we will not fear though the earth gives way, though the mountains end up in the heart of the sea.) We can find safety in the arms of our Father. He will give us strength in times of need. So we do not have to be afraid when troubles arise. We do not have to be frightened when natural disasters come. We do not have to be scared under any circumstances.

- Broad application: Fear not.
- Your application:

_____

_____

_____

_____

_____

_____

_____

_____

_____

_____

_____

_____

_____

_____

_____

_____

_____

_____

December 12:

(J) Proverbs 10:28 (The hope of the righteous brings joy, but the expectation of the wicked will perish.) As Christians, we rely on our faith in Jesus Christ as we move through life. Joy is the result of believing in the hope of eternal life. We also take great comfort in knowing that a righteous life is pleasing to our Lord. The unrighteous one has nothing to look forward to but death and destruction.

- Broad application: Jump for joy!
- Your application:

_____

_____

_____

_____

_____

_____

_____

_____

_____

_____

_____

_____

_____

_____

_____

_____

_____

_____

_____

_____

DECEMBER 13:

(L) Deuteronomy 6:4-5 ("Hear O Israel: The Lord our God, the Lord is one. You shall love the Lord your God with all your heart and with all your soul and with all your might.) There is no one like the God we serve! He is the only true God who is worthy of our love. We should love Him with all our hearts and souls. We should love Him with everything we have. We should love Him with every fiber of our being

- Broad application: Love Him like no other.
- Your application:

_____
_____
_____
_____
_____
_____
_____
_____
_____
_____
_____
_____
_____
_____
_____
_____
_____
_____
_____

DECEMBER 14:

(GO) Matthew 12:34-35 ("You brood of vipers! How can you speak well when you are evil? For out of the abundance of the heart, the mouth speaks. The good person out of his good treasure brings forth good, and the wrong person out of his evil treasure brings forth evil.") Jesus called the Pharisees vipers! They were deceitful and poisonous. He told them they couldn't speak anything good. Their hearts were full of evil. The Holy Spirit did not, could not, dwell in them.

- Broad application: Have a good heart.
- Your application:

_____
_____
_____
_____
_____
_____
_____
_____
_____
_____
_____
_____
_____
_____
_____
_____
_____
_____

DECEMBER 15:

(GE) Proverbs 14:31 (Whoever oppresses a poor man insults his Maker, but he who is generous to the needy honor him.) When we mistreat one of God's children, it is an insult to Him. He is especially hurt when it is someone in dire need. But when we help those in need, we honor Him. He finds favor in our generosity.

- Broad application: Help those in need.
- Your application:

_____

_____

_____

_____

_____

_____

_____

_____

_____

_____

_____

_____

_____

_____

_____

_____

_____

_____

_____

_____

_____

December 16:

(J) 2 Corinthians 13:11-12 (Finally, brothers, rejoice. Aim for restoration, comfort one another, agree with one another, live in peace; and the God of love and peace will be with you. Greet one another with a holy kiss.) We should be delighted! We should be glad to come together as one in Christ, greeting each other with gestures of love. We should be eager to comfort and support each other. We should want to live in harmony as God's children. That is where God's love and peace reside.

- Broad application: Get on board!
- Your application:

_____
_____
_____
_____
_____
_____
_____
_____
_____
_____
_____
_____
_____
_____
_____
_____
_____
_____

DECEMBER 17:

(L) Luke 6:27-28 ("But I say to you who hear, Love your enemies, do good to those who hate you, bless those who curse you, pray for those who abuse you.") Jesus teaches love. He instructs us to love those we see as our enemies. Jesus tells us to love those who curse us and "do good" toward them. He wants us to ask for God's favor on those who wish to harm us. He tells us we should pray for those who mistreat us.

- Broad application: Listen to the Lord.
- Your application:

_____
_____
_____
_____
_____
_____
_____
_____
_____
_____
_____
_____
_____
_____
_____
_____
_____
_____
_____
_____

December 18:

(F) Nahum 1:7 (The Lord is good, a stronghold in the day of trouble; he knows those who take refuge in him.) The Lord is good. He is a fortress for us when we are under attack. We can trust that the Lord will protect us. He knows those of us who will take refuge in Him.

- Broad application: Seek His protection.
- Your application:

_____

_____

_____

_____

_____

_____

_____

_____

_____

_____

_____

_____

_____

_____

_____

_____

_____

_____

_____

DECEMBER 19:

(F) Matthew 17:20 (He said to them, "Because of your little faith. For truly, I say to you, if you have faith like a grain of mustard seed, you will say to this mountain, 'Move from here to there,' and it will move, and nothing will be impossible for you.") Here Jesus tells His disciples they are genuinely lacking in faith. But all they needed was faith the size of a mustard seed, and they could move mountains. Nothing would be impossible. The sky is the limit!

- Broad application: Have mustard seed faith.
- Your application:

_____

_____

_____

_____

_____

_____

_____

_____

_____

_____

_____

_____

_____

_____

_____

_____

_____

DECEMBER 20:

(J) Psalm 30:11-12 (You have turned for me my mourning into dancing; you have loosed my sackcloth and clothed me with gladness, that my glory may sing your praise and not be silent. O Lord my God, I will give thanks to you forever!) There will be times in our lives when we will grieve, must grieve. But whatever the loss may be, we know God will turn that darkness into day. We will once again dance and be glad. We will not be able to hold back our joy. We will praise the Lord and glorify His name!

- Broad application: Praise Him while "going through."
- Your application:

_____
_____
_____
_____
_____
_____
_____
_____
_____
_____
_____
_____
_____
_____
_____
_____
_____

DECEMBER 21:

(L) Matthew 5:46-47 ("For if you love those who love you, what reward do you have? Do not even the tax collectors do the same? And if you greet only your brothers, what more are you doing than others? Do not even the Gentiles do the same?") It is not an incredible feat to love those who love us. Even non-Christians can do that. It is not impressive when we greet those who are just like us. Anyone who interacts with their "own kind" can do that. God's kind of impartial love is what is needed.

- Broad application: Aim higher.
- Your application:

_____
_____
_____
_____
_____
_____
_____
_____
_____
_____
_____
_____
_____
_____
_____
_____
_____
_____

DECEMBER 22:

(T) 1 Thessalonians 5:7-8 (For those who sleep, sleep at night, and those who get drunk, are drunk at night. But since we belong to the day, let us be sober, having put on the breastplate of faith and love and the hope of salvation for a helmet.) For those who use the darkness of night to sleep, we sleep. We hide in the dark of night for those who do things we know are wrong. But as Christians, we soberly walk in the light of day. Our faith and love sustain us. Our hope of salvation guides us.

- Broad application: Use daylight hours.
- Your application:

_____

_____

_____

_____

_____

_____

_____

_____

_____

_____

_____

_____

_____

_____

_____

_____

_____

_____

DECEMBER 23:

(P) Psalm 119:165 (Great peace have those who love your law; nothing can make them stumble.) Knowing the Word of God brings great peace. His Word will safeguard our steps. Stumbling and falling will not be our way of life. We can search the scriptures to use as our guide in everything we do.

- Broad application: Study His Word.
- Your application:

_____

_____

_____

_____

_____

_____

_____

_____

_____

_____

_____

_____

_____

_____

_____

_____

_____

_____

_____

_____

DECEMBER 24:

(G0) 1 Kings 15:11-12 (And Asa did what was right in the eyes of the Lord, as David his father had done. He put away the male cult prostitutes out of the land and removed all the idols that his fathers had made.) Asa was a king who did what was right in the eyes of the Lord. He was a descendant of David. He did away with all the evil that was going on before his reign. There had been a lot of idol worshipping in Judah, so he removed all the idols. He was a king in good standing with the Lord.

- Broad application: Remove your idols.
- Your application:

_____

_____

_____

_____

_____

_____

_____

_____

_____

_____

_____

_____

_____

_____

_____

_____

_____

December 25:

(J) Luke 2:10-11 (And the angel said to them, "Fear not, for behold, I bring you good news of great joy that will be for all the people. For unto you is born this day in the city of David a Savior, who is Christ the Lord.") The angel wanted the shepherds to know there was no need to be afraid. He was bringing only good news, great news. A Savior, Christ the Lord, would be born on this day! It was a joyous occasion then. It remains a joyous occasion today.

- Broad application: Take delight in that day!
- Your application:

_____

_____

_____

_____

_____

_____

_____

_____

_____

_____

_____

_____

_____

_____

_____

_____

DECEMBER 26:

(L) 1 Peter 1:18-19 (Knowing Jesus bought us from the futile ways inherited from your forefathers, not with perishable things such as silver or gold, but with the precious blood of Christ, like that of a lamb without blemish or spot.) Jesus did not buy us with mere silver or gold. He paid with something more precious than that. The blood of Jesus was the only thing that could redeem us. It was the only thing pure enough. Jesus paid the perfect price.

- Broad application: Appreciate the cost.
- Your application:

_____

_____

_____

_____

_____

_____

_____

_____

_____

_____

_____

_____

_____

_____

_____

_____

_____

_____

_____

DECEMBER 27:

(P) Psalm 27:1-2 (The Lord is my light and my salvation; whom shall I fear? The Lord is the stronghold of my life; of whom shall I be afraid? When evildoers assail me to eat up my flesh, my adversaries and foes, it is they who stumble and fall.) Jesus is the light. He is the way to our salvation. Knowing this, we should be at peace and not be afraid. He is our protection against the evil ones. They will not prevail.

- Broad application: Stay close to the light.
- Your application:

_____

_____

_____

_____

_____

_____

_____

_____

_____

_____

_____

_____

_____

_____

_____

_____

_____

_____

DECEMBER 28:

(J) Luke 19:37-38 (As Jesus was on his way down the Mount of Olives, all his disciples began to rejoice and praise God for the mighty works they had seen. They said, "Blessed is the King who comes in the name of the Lord! Peace in heaven and glory in the highest!") The crowd went wild! They were singing God's praises! They were thrilled to know the Father had sent His Son Jesus to perform such miracles! He had just given sight to the blind and raised Lazarus from the dead. There was peace in heaven, glory in the highest!

- Broad application: Remember your miracles!
- Your application:

_____

_____

_____

_____

_____

_____

_____

_____

_____

_____

_____

_____

_____

_____

_____

_____

_____

December 29:

(L) Ezekiel 22:29-30 (The people of the land have practiced extortion and committed robbery. They have oppressed the poor and needy and have extorted from the sojourner without justice. And I sought for a man among them who should build up the wall and stand in the breach before me for the land, that I should not destroy it, but I found none.) Jerusalem was full of sinful people and sinful acts at this time. People were being robbed and misused. God was looking for anyone to stand up and do the right thing. He needed someone to show love for his fellow man. There was none, not one.

- Broad application: Stand up for what's right.
- Your application:

_____
_____
_____
_____
_____
_____
_____
_____
_____
_____
_____
_____
_____
_____
_____

DECEMBER 30:

(F) 1 Timothy 3:16 (Great indeed, we confess, is the mystery of godliness: He was manifested in the flesh, vindicated by the Spirit, seen by angels, proclaimed among the nations, believed in the world, taken up in glory.) Our faith relies on the beautiful mystery of our Lord and Savio,r Jesus Christ. He came in the flesh, but He was made righteous by the Spirit. When Jesus walked the earth, angels saw that Jesus preached the gospel, and the people accepted it. He was then taken back to glory.

- Broad application: Simply believe the mystery.
- Your application:

_____

_____

_____

_____

_____

_____

_____

_____

_____

_____

_____

_____

_____

_____

_____

_____

_____

_____

December 31:

(GO) Luke 6:37-38 ("Do not judge, and people will not judge you. Do not condemn, and people will not condemn you. Forgive, and people will forgive you. Give, and people will give to you. Good measure pressed down, shaken together, running over, is yours. For with the measure you use, you will get it back.") To judge or carefully consider is not a sin. But it is when it comes to condemnation. The fate of all of us is in the capable hands of the Lord. We should extend forgiveness to others and be of service to others. And when we give our "good measure" toward others, it will be returned to us "beyond measure."

- Broad application: Do unto others...
- Your application:

_____

_____

_____

_____

_____

_____

_____

_____

_____

_____

_____

_____

_____

_____

_____

_____

CPSIA information can be obtained
at www.ICGtesting.com
Printed in the USA
BVHW041606170223
658752BV00002B/2

9 781662 869372